RESCUE

TRUE STORIES FROM CLARK COUNTY, WA

Published in Beaverton, Oregon, by Good Catch Publishing.
www.goodcatchpublishing.com
V1.1

Printed in the United States of America

TABLE OF CONTENTS

DEDICATION

This book is dedicated to the individuals who appear in its pages, who had the courage to "lay it all on the table," so to speak, with soul-level transparency. We believe that no pain is wasted and that the triumph and hope these individuals have experienced can be multiplied in the lives of those who read this book.

ACKNOWLEDGEMENTS

I would like to thank Bill Courtnay for his vision for this book and Tiffany Seppala for her hard work in making it a reality. To those who shared their personal stories in this book, thank you for your boldness and vulnerability.

This book would not have been published without the amazing efforts of our project manager and editor, Hayley Pandolph. Her untiring resolve pushed this project forward and turned it into a stunning victory. Thank you for your great fortitude and diligence. Deep thanks to our incredible editor in chief, Michelle Cuthrell, and executive editor, Jen Genovesi, for all the amazing work they do. I would also like to thank our invaluable proofreader, Melody Davis, for the focus and energy she puts into perfecting our words.

Lastly, I want to extend our gratitude to the creative and very talented Shawnie Aho, who designed the beautiful cover for *Rescue: True Stories from Clark County, WA*.

Daren Lindley
President and CEO
Good Catch Publishing

The book you are about to read
is a compilation of authentic life stories.
The facts are true, and the events are real.
These storytellers have dealt with crisis, tragedy, abuse
and neglect and have shared their most private moments,
mess-ups and hang-ups in order for others to learn and
grow from them. In order to protect the identities of those
involved in their pasts, the names and details of some
storytellers have been withheld or changed.

INTRODUCTION

What do you do when life careens out of control? When addiction overtakes you or abuse chains you with fear? Is depression escapable? Will relationships ever be healthy again? Are we destined to dissolve into an abyss of sorrow? Or will the sunlight of happiness ever return?

Your life really can change. It is possible to become a new person. The stories you are about to read prove positively that people right here in Clark County have stopped dying and started living. Whether you've been beaten by abuse, broken promises, shattered dreams or suffocating addictions, the resounding answer is, "Yes! You can become a new person." The potential to break free from gloom and into a bright future awaits.

Expect inspiration, hope and transformation! As you walk with these real people from our very own neighborhoods through the pages of this book, you will not only find riveting accounts of their hardships, you will learn the secrets that brought about their breakthroughs. These people are no longer living in the shadows of yesterday; they are thriving with a sense of mission and purpose TODAY. May these stories inspire you to do the same.

DARKNESS LURKING
THE STORY OF WAYNE
WRITTEN BY MARY WAHL

"Quick! Somebody call 911!"

I climbed into the boat.

"911. What's your emergency?"

My mind went blank. How could I describe where I was and which way the water flowed? I panicked. We had to find her. I strained to see something, anything — but I couldn't see a thing. Darkness slowly crept over the horizon, and I could do nothing to stop it.

ૹૹૹ

"Congratulations, Mr. and Mrs. Smith. It's a boy."

I was my parents' second son, followed by two more brothers and two sisters — six in all.

In my early childhood, we moved to a spacious, beautiful, cozy log cabin in Rindge, New Hampshire. My dad worked in construction and imported our cabin from Finland.

Each season, winter, spring, summer or fall, displayed its own beauty. Often, the sun shone brightly through the tall birch trees that surrounded our cabin. Years later, I can close my eyes and still see and smell smoke rising from the rock chimney on those cold, brisk days as the leaves began to change.

RESCUE

Often, my family and I gathered around the fireplace in the evenings. Mom sang and wrote her own country songs, and I loved listening to her beautiful melodies. The notes she sang floated up through the vaulted ceiling of our log cabin.

৵৵৵

We spent our summers at Granite Lake near Keene, New Hampshire.

"Race you to the island!" my oldest brother, Rick, taunted me.

"Race on," I retorted.

I looked out over the lake and saw our paddle boats tied to the nearest dock. We each climbed into our own boat.

"On your mark, get set, GO!" we shouted.

We paddled our way to the middle of the island on Granite Lake.

"I won!" Rick teased.

Once on the island, I looked for the biggest and juiciest blueberries to plop into my pail. I couldn't wait to taste the homemade pancakes Mom made with our fresh-picked fruit.

My siblings, cousins and I spent countless summer nights swimming in the lake. We would jump off the dock at the same time and splash into the cool water. Shivering, we would run to the hot, steamy sauna, and once our bodies warmed, we would jump into the lake again. I loved those days because they were filled with sunshine, laughter and evenings hanging out with my aunts and uncles, cousins, siblings and Dad and Mom. I remember endless hours of fun, no matter what the season.

"That's perfect!" I shouted to my brothers one morning.

Rick and Steve found a whole stack of two-by-fours, and we set off to find a box of nails to build a fort. Dad's work in construction provided us plenty of scrap materials.

I loved to build forts, whether by myself or with my siblings or cousins. I felt safe in them and would go there whenever I got upset. But some pain I just couldn't hide from — not even in my best fort.

❧❧❧❧

"Mrs. Smith," the doctor said. "I am sorry to tell you that your test results have come back positive. You have Leukemia."

At 11, I didn't understand what this meant. Because of an economic downturn, we had moved to Ironwood, Michigan. Mom's sister, Aunt Carolyn, rented us an older house with a barn off to the side.

Mom started her chemo treatments and began to lose her hair. At first I was shocked when I witnessed Mom losing all of her hair, but in time the initial shock wore off.

Regular visits to the doctor became a big part of our lives. With the optimism of a child, I felt certain she would get better soon, and life would go on like normal.

As a family, we regularly attended church. Dad and Mom believed God was real. Their confidence in God helped them get through her illness by trusting in him for the strength to make it through, day by day. However, I still had a lot to learn about this kind of trust.

ॐॐॐ

My extended family learned about Mom's sickness.

"We're coming to help you and take care of the kids during this time," Aunt Suzie told Mom over the phone.

A couple days later, she and my uncle arrived. Later in the week, Uncle Bob gathered all six of us and took us to the store.

"Pick out any mountain bike you want," he said.

Our eyes grew big with excitement. Although we all chose different colors, that day we each picked out our own 21-speed mountain bike.

Doing the things I loved represented my picture of a perfect childhood. Whether riding my bike, exploring, building forts, playing in the water or in the snow, I loved to engage in outdoor activities. I was sure Mom would get better and life would go on as normal. Soon, Mom went into remission, and the days felt carefree again.

"Let's go to The Term," one of my siblings suggested one day.

We hopped on our bikes and rode over to a place called "The Term." We lived near a small airport, and "The Term" offered us a place to munch on a candy bar and enjoy a soft drink.

DARKNESS LURKING

In winter, we also found plenty of things to do.

"Score! We won!" my brothers and sisters yelled.

And with that, our game of ice hockey ended.

Other times, when the ice was thick enough to hold us, we put on old ice skates and skated on the pond. Even though we bundled up with coats, hats and scarves, our fingers began tingling. When we could take the cold no longer, we sat in the warming hut in the middle of the island.

No matter where we lived, there were always plenty of places for a young boy to explore.

≈≈≈

Months passed. Mom felt better, and the economy started to look up. Dad and Mom decided to move to Simpsonville, South Carolina. South Carolina proved a whole new world for me and my brothers and sisters to discover.

One day, we found kudzu vines thick enough to make into swings and discovered old rock bridges. Some days, Mom would make us sack lunches, and we'd set off to have a picnic on an old rock bridge near a stream.

Although we lived in South Carolina, we still spent summers in New Hampshire with family. Everything in my short life seemed perfect and going my way.

As was tradition every summer, my family joined together for a BBQ and lobster fest at my aunt and uncle's house. My cousins and I laughed hysterically.

"Run!" I would say.

We ran from the pool to the hill, where we cheered on our frog in the frog-hopping competition, and spent hours watching magicians perform.

"I am hungry!" one of us exclaimed.

We worked up an appetite, and drawn by the wonderful smell of food, we plopped into a seat under a big white tent. I ate every last bite of my chicken and corn on the cob. I felt a tap on my shoulder.

"Come with us a minute." Dad and Mom gathered up all six of us kids.

My brothers and sisters and I followed Dad and Mom into an office. One by one, we sat down.

Dad cleared his throat and said, "Your mom has a really bad sore throat … and we have to get her to the hospital right away."

Mom's Leukemia had returned, this time with a vengeance. They told us of their immediate plans to head to the hospital. The music outside seemed to fade away.

かかか

Eventually, we got the call that we needed to visit Mom in the hospital and say our goodbyes. Totally numb, I walked into her hospital room and clung to her.

How does a 14-year-old boy say goodbye to his mom? I still wanted to say so much more. More that I wanted to show her. I wanted her to experience more of my life.

I longed to spend just one more day with her.

DARKNESS LURKING

That night, Aunt Suzie came to the basement where I slept. She quietly leaned over and whispered in my ear, "Wayne, your mom has passed away." I sat up and rubbed my eyes. Although her voice was soft, her words screamed in my head. I heard her screaming that Mom, although she had put up an incredible fight, had lost her battle.

☙☙☙

Numbness completely took over my body as we laid Mom to rest. I walked around in a daze. I put on a fake smile, a mask, and pretended I was okay. People came to celebrate her life.

Acquaintances and strangers alike hugged me and said, "So sorry for your loss, son."

Deep down inside, a huge void formed, an unfamiliar darkness nobody else could see. From that day on, I began to emotionally distance myself from others.

I remember the overcast sky on the day we laid Mom to rest. The graveside service had begun, and I found myself standing in a sheer fog. As we sang the last song and uttered the final tribute, all those gathered around noticed multiple rainbows in the sky.

Bittersweet.

But what a beautiful tribute to Mom.

☙☙☙

In the days that followed, I continued to stuff my pain. The darkness in me grew too vast to confront. We never returned to South Carolina. My cousins went there for us, packed up all our stuff and brought it back to New Hampshire.

Life was chaotic. My dad did his best to keep us kids together. All my family members jumped in to help in any way that they could.

と と と

The year I turned 15, Dad decided to move to Washington. Again, we lived with family. In time, Dad remarried. Our new stepmom loved to help others, and she fit right into our family. Life appeared to be getting to a new kind of normal. Our lives seemed to be getting into a rhythm.

In the summer I turned 17, we went boating on the Willamette River. I felt the cool water splash my face. I felt the wakeboard slip from under my feet. I fell off and waited for the boat to come back and pick me up.

As I waited, I heard Aunt Emily and Uncle Sean screaming, "Help!" Then, "Somebody call 911!"

A lot of kids were on the boat, including my 5-year-old cousin, Olivia. Before anyone on the boat could even blink twice, Olivia had gotten too close to the edge at the back, flipped off and likely hit her head on the boat.

"Oh, God!" my aunt and uncle shouted. "Why aren't you saving us?"

I started swimming back to the boat. Uncle Sean and other family members dove into the river desperately looking for any sign of Olivia.

My hands trembled as I climbed back into the boat. We searched and searched the surrounding water, but never found Olivia.

"911. What's your emergency?" I felt a huge lump in my throat as I explained the scene.

Doing their best to locate us, they asked me, "What do you see? Which way is the water flowing?"

The familiar pain, the void, the darkness, gripped me.

Hours later, the grief counselor at the hospital told me words I will never forget.

"Son, accidents are nobody's fault."

I knew what came next — the funeral, tears of sadness, memories shared, people gathered round to express their love for my family and my precious little cousin.

రారారా

Sometime after Olivia's funeral, I put on my all-too-familiar mask and stuffed the pain way down. Desperate to find something that would numb my pain, I started partying with my buddies and a cousin of mine.

The smoke from the weed rose into the air — we knew how to have a good ole' time, hanging out together in a vacant trailer. But in time, the laughter faded, and when I looked over, my buddies were passed out.

The room began to spin, and I heard more laughing,

but the laughs grew deeper and more sinister. Out of the blue, it seemed like a dark shadow, a big creature, crept toward me and reached out to grab me. I felt all alone and petrified.

"Jesus!" I instinctively cried.

In an instant, my eyes grew big as I saw a beam of light — something like a shooting star — hit the shadowy creature. The shadowy creature ran away, and I looked up into a nearby tree and saw a beautiful angelic being.

Even after such a terrifying first experience, alcohol and drugs became a normal part of my life.

৵৵৵

One day, I remember talking to a therapist about my dark feelings and my fear of being swallowed up by darkness. Up until that point in my life, I hadn't talked about any of my pain. In a way, I believed that the darkness was a part of me.

"Oh, no," the therapist said. "The darkness is the grief that is desperately trying to claw its way out."

At the time, her words made some sense, and I knew I desperately wanted to make some changes in my life.

৵৵৵

I graduated from high school and still partied hard, but I tried to clean up my act. Even some of my buddies tried to quit, but inevitably one of us would start again, and the rest of us would follow. During that time, I held down a job and lived in a two-bedroom apartment with seven buddies.

One night, we took Ecstasy and sat on the back patio, higher than a kite.

"Yo, man," my good friend Neil yelled. "It looks like your hair is on fire!"

We all laughed. Soon, one by one, all of my buddies began to pass out. I started to hallucinate. On the back wall, an arm on a poster reached out to grab me. Certain I was completely surrounded by darkness and dark creatures, I dropped to the ground and curled up in a ball.

I hallucinated that I held a ball of light and one of the creatures, and then another, would try to grasp it saying, "Drop it. Let go of it."

Looking back, I believe that ball of light was faith.

Even though I felt like I had nothing left, as if I were the end of a cigarette butt, there was still a small bit of ash left. I started to sing a song I learned as a young boy, "Jesus Loves Me." No matter the struggle, no matter the tricks the creatures or my mind tried to play on me, I would not let go of the ball.

⌒⌒⌒

When I turned 21, I married a beautiful girl, Janet. Together, we partied from time to time. However, I knew that in order to make some positive changes in my life, the time had come for us to move. We moved into a different apartment in Battle Ground, Washington. Life began to look up.

"He's got your eyes," my wife exclaimed. Our first son, Joshua, brought a smile no one on earth could erase. Before we knew it, Joshua turned 2.

My wife surprised me one day. "Honey, I am pregnant again!"

Excitement welled up within both of us as we anticipated our baby's arrival. Janet was 20 weeks along. Our midwife came into her bedroom at our house to start the ultrasound. We could not wait to hear the heartbeat and see our baby.

As she waved the wand around, we saw fingers and toes but realized our baby wasn't moving. Janet and I found ourselves in complete and utter shock. The grief, the all-too-familiar darkness, grabbed us around our necks and would not let go.

My wife had wanted to deliver our baby at home. Labor was induced, and the bittersweet moment came when we laid eyes on and held our son for the first and last time. The funeral took place at my dad's house, and my father-in-law built a mini-casket for our baby. That day, we laid our sweet baby boy to rest under a tree. The pain of loss was familiar by now.

And I wanted, once again, to numb my pain. One night, I saw my wife's huge bottle of morphine pills. She would take one-fourth to one-half of a pill as her body recovered. By this time, I had become an expert at hiding. I looked at the bottle and took one pill. Then, in time, two pills. I worked my way up to sometimes five pills at a time. I began to party harder — anything to numb my pain.

One evening, I noticed that she was running out of pain pills.

What am I going to do now?

Scared and alone, I convinced myself to start weaning my body off of them. The last night, without any more pills to take, I began to sweat one minute and shiver the next. I explained my behavior away by telling my wife I had the flu.

Still hiding the truth.

කිකිකි

One afternoon, the phone rang.

"Hello, Wayne." It was Aunt Heather. "Sean and I really want you to come to Church on the Rock family camp."

As newlyweds, we'd often been invited by my parents to Church on the Rock. We attended church with them about once a month. But by this time, we had three children: Joshua, Sophia and Cole. I wanted nothing to do with God or church. *If he truly cared, why would he let me experience such excruciating loss, so many people I loved?*

I hesitated and tried to think of every excuse not to go. However, no excuse worked. I finally decided to try camp one time.

කිකිකි

Once at camp, I could have gone home at any point, but something compelled me to stay.

Am I crazy?

Feeling horrible and like my throat was on fire, I went into the bathroom and began to cry out to God.

I felt like God heard my cry and told me, *It is through being vulnerable, letting your wife and parents see into the real you, that I will bring healing to your years of pain.*

I walked out of the bathroom looking for Janet and my parents. I unloaded everything that I had pent up inside of me for years. It felt good to finally be real and let them see me — the hurt, the anger, the tears, the loneliness, the addictions, the dark grief that had been a constant companion, a shadow lurking over my life.

As I revealed the truth, I felt a huge weight lift from my shoulders. Janet and my parents provided a safe place for me. I believe that Jesus was showing his love and acceptance through them.

At the church I grew up in, I learned about Jesus and how much he loved me. I even told Jesus I wanted him to be a part of my life. But it wasn't until that moment when I laid it all bare before Janet and my parents that I truly understood that Jesus had suffered and died for *me* and that his power could change my life if I surrendered to him. He wasn't just someone up there watching from a distance. No, I finally believed that Jesus had been watching over me at all times, during the good times and the ones I couldn't bear on my own.

Mom wrote a prayerful song called "Watch Over My

Children," with tender words: "With your great love, keep them from harm; hold them in your arms along the way." Her words moved me because I had lived them. Countless times I should have been dead, but because of his continual love and care for me, God watched over me. God definitely answered the cry of Mom's heart. Jesus healed me from my brokenness and pain.

As I sat at camp and listened to the powerful stories told by a pastor from Sri Lanka, Jesus' love for me became more real, and my confidence in God grew stronger. I was sprinkled with water in baptism as an infant, but as I took in story after story about the love of Jesus, I decided to be immersed in the lake at camp. I wanted to make it known to those around me that the love of Jesus had forever changed me — that he had brought me from darkness into light.

With the sun about to set, I waited on the beach, ready to get into the water. Pastor Brian, the pastor of Church on the Rock, stood waiting for me. I looked up on the hillside and saw my family and all the caring people from Church on the Rock. As Pastor Brian dipped me under the water and I came back up, I heard clapping and cheering — celebration! I began to celebrate, too, because it dawned on me that no strings were attached to God's love. And I realized that Jesus IS real. For years, I had been carrying around garbage and had a hard, calloused heart, but God broke through.

෴ ෴ ෴

RESCUE

After family camp, Janet and I fell on some harder times financially, and we moved in with my dad and stepmom. Learning to trust God to take care of me proved to be a new experience, but I chose to trust that God would provide exactly what we needed. And provide he did.

One Sunday, on our way to Church on the Rock, my wife and I were praying about the need for a bike. Our son Joshua's birthday was coming up, and we did not have enough money to buy him one.

While we walked out of church that day, a complete stranger stopped us.

She asked, "Does your son have a bike? My son just outgrew a brand-new bike. I would like to give it to you."

Janet and I stood there stunned. Tears of thankfulness filled our eyes. God used a complete stranger to provide. I learned that day that God does answer prayer, and he cares for every detail of our lives.

এঔএঔএঔ

I have learned that life is fragile. It is a gift and not to be taken for granted. I have found ways that I can help others benefit from the lessons I learned the hard way.

I believe the prayers Mom prayed years ago are still being answered today. I believe God's protection has been over me from the moment I took my first breath and will be until the moment I take my last. One day, I believe, I will be reunited with her, Olivia and our precious baby boy. God has heard my cry through every season of life: as a young boy, a teenager, young adult and an adult.

He pierced through my darkness and brought me to his incredible light.

STRIPPING THE PAINTED HOUSE
THE STORY OF DAISY
WRITTEN BY ROSEMARIE FITZSIMMONS

From the outside, nobody could tell it was a house of pain. The two-story five-bedroom home looked joyful, with its moss-green siding and orange trim (leftovers from my uncle's summer paint jobs) and a large white front porch that suggested welcome.

How easily people can be fooled by a coat of paint.

For as long as I could remember, my heartbeat quickened and my pace slowed every time I rounded the corner in front of that house. Then a knot would form in my stomach at the start of the concrete walkway and tighten with each lead-weight step I took toward those wooden stairs.

My siblings and I never knew what we'd be walking into or how soon the shouting would start. We didn't know whether we'd be abruptly sent off to a friend's house to spend the night or, worse, "visited" in the early morning hours.

One day was different. One day we dared to hope.

It was late on a Sunday morning, and as my four siblings and I rounded the corner, we walked in a close huddle behind Mom up the steps and toward the door, a cautious excitement brewing in our bellies.

"Is he gone?" little Jemmy whispered, taking my hand.

"Hush, Jemmy," said Kyle, the oldest. "If he ain't, we don't wanna make him mad."

My mother said nothing. She took a deep breath before turning the knob and stepped into the house ahead of us. One by one, we scooted past her, fanning out to walk through the rooms, each taking a wide-eyed inventory as we made our rounds. Our shouts echoed off the empty hardwood floors.

"His books are gone!"

"So are his record albums!"

"Clothes, too. Closet's empty!"

As I watched my mother exhale, relief washed over me. He was gone. He wasn't coming back. Liberation Day! He would no longer manipulate and control my life. At age 9, for the first time, I could tell my mom the secrets he made me swear never to tell. It took me an hour or so to muster my courage, but I just couldn't let another day pass without telling her.

I found her sitting on the end of her bed, one hand on her forehead. I entered the room, stood in front of her and just started talking. She listened quietly, her brown eyes boring into me as I poured out everything I could remember about how he had touched me again and again. Mercifully, I couldn't recall the toddler years.

"I knew it was wrong, Mommy. I kept telling him it was wrong, but he just didn't care."

To my great relief, she believed me, and she promised to "take care of this." It never occurred to me to wonder why she didn't seem surprised.

STRIPPING THE PAINTED HOUSE

After he went to jail, I thought, *I'm safe now,* and I was grateful that my mother had taken my burden away from me.

What I didn't know, however, was that my burden was too large for her to carry.

Nor did I know that a new tormentor was taking up residence in my mind and in my heart and that the next battle would be even greater.

���

My real father died before I was born. At 63, he was 33 years older than Mom when she became pregnant with me, her third child. He started experiencing chest pains during Lamaze classes one day, and the next day he was gone. Massive heart attack, the doctors said. My mother was devastated. He'd always taken care of her — she didn't know how she could possibly cope without him.

They met when she was 20 at a Bible study hosted by her parents. He'd served in the Navy, worked as a municipal judge and already raised one family.

Mom married him when she was 25, and his death devastated her. Her whole life, she'd been well sheltered; there had always been a man around to take care of her.

I was only a year old when Mom met Ken. I can't say I blame her for letting him into our lives. She was a widow with three young children to care for. Ken brought stability, companionship and a paycheck.

He also brought violence and abuse.

RESCUE

I knew I could never tell Mom what went on in that house when she was away or sometimes while she slept. I kept it to myself and did my best to appear "normal," even to the kids at school. I couldn't bear the idea of them looking at me in that *knowing* way, so I dealt with it. Shoved it down and painted myself over like the welcoming porch.

Our house was in constant chaos and not just because there was only one bathroom for seven people. Fighting began the moment Ken walked in the door. Mom took a lot. Sometimes the five of us were caught in the crossfire. We learned to stay low and share little.

After Ken left for good and Mom divorced him, I thought our relationship would improve, that her anger would subside. It didn't. She'd take us to church, where we'd learn love and forgiveness, but then we'd return to a home with neither. She criticized us constantly, and it seemed we could never please her. We never talked about the hurt.

"Quit being so thin-skinned," she'd say when I'd bring it up. "The world isn't fair. You have to pull yourself up by your own boot straps."

Mom did arrange some counseling. I remember being told, "It's okay to be angry at him." But I wasn't angry. Confused, frustrated, guilty and ashamed, yes, but not angry. She didn't tell me what to do about guilt and shame, so I left them inside — kept the porch looking nice. I wouldn't be labeled a victim, so I labeled myself a "Not a Victim."

STRIPPING THE PAINTED HOUSE

Over the next eight years, I wanted desperately to feel loved. I had no idea what love felt like, but I wanted it. I kissed a boy on the cheek when I was 9, and I always had some sort of "relationship" with someone. I started flirting at school and at our church youth group. I knew exactly how to get a boy's attention. I giggled at inappropriate jokes and contributed some of my own. I said what I thought people wanted me to say, and they responded the way I expected them to.

One Sunday, I was sitting in church with my family when the preacher gave an especially rousing talk and encouraged anyone who wanted to "give his or her life" to Jesus to come forward. I found myself moving up the aisle, almost on autopilot. I so wanted to know this Jesus he spoke of. I stood at the front of the church with some other people while the preacher prayed over us.

Tears streamed down my face, and I knew in my heart something had changed. In fact, I'm sure I did change, but my behavior did not. I continued to flirt.

Home life continued to worsen. Mom and I fought, mostly over boys.

When I was 16 and I met Tom, she launched into a tirade on all the reasons she didn't approve.

"Stay away from him," she yelled. "You're going to get hurt!"

"Don't worry," I shouted back, knowing exactly which buttons to push, "I'm not planning to marry him. I just want to make out with him!"

She infuriated me. I dreamt of the day I'd leave home.

I would find a man who loved me, and we would live in a beautiful home, happily ever after. That would show her.

ॐॐॐ

"If you really loved me, you'd let me."

We'd been through this so many times it was like an old television rerun. I was 17 and mesmerized by Tom's blue-green eyes. He was so good-looking. We hadn't even known each other a year, but I wanted desperately to believe he loved me. He was 20 and had already fathered a daughter. I knew many other women found him attractive, but he had chosen me. That had to count for something.

"I can't, Tom. My mother would kill me."

"She doesn't have to know."

"Oh, she'll know. And besides, it's wrong."

"Not if we really love each other."

He gave me a smoldering look that said, "I'm not waiting forever, you know."

I couldn't bear it if he found someone else. I needed him to love me. Besides, if he left me, I thought, I'd be a victim, and I certainly wasn't that. He wore his ratty green ball cap backward over his blond hair. It made him look carefree — it accentuated the green in his eyes. When he looked at me like that …

"Okay," I said. "Where should we go?"

We thought we loved each other, but we didn't begin to understand the difference between sex and love. We didn't understand the depth of abuse we'd each experienced — his an entirely different type than mine. We both came from single-mom households and extreme poverty. Each of us thought we'd found what we needed in the other. We didn't have a clue.

ତ୍ୟତ୍ୟତ୍ୟ

It hadn't even occurred to me that I might be pregnant. I'd gone to the clinic for a pelvic infection, and someone on the staff asked if they could run a pregnancy test. Just like that, my world changed. I was alone, shocked, scared. For a while, all I could do was cry. Although I still lived at home, I couldn't tell Mom.

Tom took the news well. In fact, he seemed pleased and even excited. I started to believe everything might be all right. I moved into Tom's place because it seemed like the right thing to do.

I may be pregnant, but I'm a good girl. Living with him will at least make me look legitimate.

I dropped out of youth group, but I continued to attend church on Sundays. I believed that the truth could be found there somewhere, even though my circumstances didn't coincide with my beliefs. One Sunday, we read a story from the Bible (John 6) in which many followers were leaving Jesus, and he asked his 12 disciples if they wanted to leave, also. Peter answered, "Where else can we go? You have the words of eternal life." Peter's words resonated in my heart. I understood exactly what he meant because I felt the same way. I felt as if church was the only place I *could* go. Even though I'd strayed so far off course, I still tried to follow God in some version of what I thought was right.

I also knew I was tough — tougher than my mom. I vowed not to make the mistakes she made. I could pull myself up by my own boot straps. I would be a *good* mother, a Not-a-Victim mother.

That's about the time the pretty paint on my house started to peel.

ॐॐॐ

"You know," said Kyle, "Mom knew about the abuse long before she kicked Ken out. He went to jail for it when you were a toddler."

"You're lying," I said. "She would never have let him do that."

We were just hanging out on my back porch, talking about the past — trouble we got into, friends who'd moved away — nothing serious, and then, *bam!*

I could only stare at him.

"She caught him doing something." Kyle's eyes met mine. "I don't know what — she never talked about it. Next thing we knew, he was gone."

I searched his face for any sign of kidding but saw none.

"Then why did she let him come back in the house?"

"I don't know." Kyle's gaze dropped. "He'd served a

year in jail. Came back apologizing and begging for forgiveness — said he'd changed his ways, and she believed him."

"I remember nothing."

"Well, you were too young to know what was going on. I was 7. I remember like it was yesterday."

"But why would she — I guess I just can't believe she'd leave me, or any of us, alone with him. I would think she'd watch him like a hawk."

"I don't know." Kyle scowled. "He was a lot more careful after that. I don't think she ever caught him again. I used to think she *must* have figured it out … I just don't know."

This couldn't be happening.

I went over to Mom's house to confront her. I wanted so desperately for her to deny everything, but she didn't. Instead she said she'd believed his story and that he'd changed.

"I did the best I could have done in my situation," she said. "That was 10 years ago. I don't know why you have to be so sensitive about it *now*."

Her words landed like a kick to the gut.

This betrayal hurt much more than anything Ken had ever done. Him, I could forgive. He was broken. In pulling myself up, I'd somehow erased those memories and moved forward. I considered my memory block a blessing. It made forgiving a broken man easier.

But until that conversation with my brother, I'd believed Mom had done all she could to keep me safe, and that talk with her 9-year-old daughter on Liberation Day had been the first she'd ever heard of the abuse.

Now it became clear: She not only knew about the abuse, but she held the door open for it to continue. I felt like an orphan.

Bitterness began to creep into my heart. I couldn't help but compare myself to Russell Crowe's character, John Nash, in *A Beautiful Mind*, who said, "Despite my … upbringing, I'm actually quite well-balanced — I have a chip on both shoulders."

But I was the tough one. I refused to be a victim. I lifted those boot straps again and moved forward with two giant chips on my shoulders. I called them "Not a Victim" and "How dare you do this to me?"

Repainting my house with my own strength was becoming a major chore.

ॐॐॐ

In October, two months after I turned 18, Tom and I married. Our daughter Melanie had just turned a month old. When Melanie was 2, I gave birth to Bethany and then, only 14 months later, to Caroline.

Our lives settled into a chaotic, stressful pattern. But as long as the chaos continued, I could function from day to day because I never had time to think. It was one task after another. We moved about 12 times in five years. Tom would find work and be content for three months or so, then he'd quit for a "better paying" job elsewhere, and we'd move to be close to his work site. The paltry pay increases never covered expenses. We had an unreliable car that constantly broke down, and his child support to pay, so we struggled to make ends meet.

We still went to church because that's what people did. I did not blame God for my chaos. I believed I'd made my bed with my decisions, and therefore, I had to lie in it. I also considered the chaos we lived in normal. I figured all new moms were overwhelmed and borderline hysterical.

So, not willing to be the victim, I pulled myself up, repainted my house Happy-New-Mom-Cheerful, and I dealt with it.

The chaos began to ebb when I was about 23. We moved into the apartment we'd live in for the next five years, and for the first time in my adult life, the pace slowed, a routine began to settle around me and I had more time to think. That's when my depression started.

I didn't know how to be alone. I had three kids under age 5, including a newborn, and no help. I didn't have the kind of relationship with my mother where I could ask for help. When she did visit, all she offered was criticism. It hurt the most when she called me overprotective.

I did have two close friends, both married with kids. For a while they offered me glimpses of what I considered normalcy. Then both of them had affairs at the same time, got pregnant from the affairs and both gave their babies up for adoption. I decided we had nothing in common and walked away from those relationships and further into loneliness.

Tom had been injured at work and placed on medical disability, and he was dealing with issues of his own. He couldn't help.

When I told people I was lonely, they'd scoff, "Nonsense! How can you be lonely when you're married?"

Trust me, it's possible.

I took Caroline to the clinic one day for a new-baby check, and while answering questions for the nurse, I found myself telling her that our electricity had been turned off that morning. Before I knew it, my list of woes started spilling over like a waterfall.

She put her hand on my shoulder and said, "Girl, I think you might be in a depression."

I practically laughed in my hysteria. "Ya think?"

But I didn't really take her seriously. I figured depression was just another term for hard life — a mother's lot. Life is hard. Duh. Get over it.

Stop being so sensitive.

Depression started with the little things. I became forgetful, unable to think clearly, and yet, I thought constantly. I brooded over those girlhood dreams about who I was going to be and how starkly they clashed with the reality of who I'd become.

How did I go so far astray in just a few years?

I'd always seen myself as someone who overcame abuse and rose above it. My victory defined me, and I thought I'd left all my ugly baggage with other people along the way. But as I looked at my life, I started to realize that I still had every bag with me and had dealt with exactly nothing, except to paint over the mess (although, in a drab color) so that nobody had to look at it.

The burden became unbearable — I'd swapped physical chaos for emotional chaos.

Not that anyone could tell. I never cried in public. I was so proud to be tough and not like one of those needy girls that I developed a gruff persona. When I'd listen to someone's painful story, I'd think things like, *What? That's all you've got? That's nothing. You have no idea what hardship is.*

And when they cried, my face would say, *You poor dear,* while my heart shouted, *Get over it. Pull yourself up, and move on. I did it, and so can you.*

I threw myself into activity, defining my worth and identity by what I did or, more accurately, by what others saw me doing. I painted my face Kind and Generous and just got busy; one year I hand-sewed Christmas gifts for everyone in Tom's family and mine. At church I sang on the worship team, led the moms' group and directed the Vacation Bible School program. I coordinated large events and weddings, and I often made elaborate wedding cakes — anything to prove my value. People just knew that if they needed something, I could make it happen. I was proud of that, and I soaked up their gratitude and approval. On the flip side, I did not feel kind at all. Because I operated out of a sense of need and not generosity, I wasn't the ideal person to work with, and I'm sure I made many people feel judged and criticized.

Then the depression became crippling, and I had to start saying no. When the holidays rolled around again, I couldn't even *shop* for Christmas gifts, let alone make them. I started turning down requests to do tasks I'd once considered easy; they'd become nearly impossible because just doing took too much energy. The approval stopped flowing.

I changed in the way I treated people and how I felt about them. We stayed involved in the church and attended faithfully, so despite my loneliness, I often found myself surrounded by people. My skin would actually hurt when they came near; I didn't want to interact, but I had this persona to display of the faithful, helpful survivor.

Jamie led a crafts ministry at our church, and I truly loved her. One day while helping her prepare for a class, I thought I was being inspirational when I picked up a project and said, "Oh, wow, this craft has so far to go!"

I waited expectantly for her to ask what it needed; I had many ideas for improvement. Instead, she said, "Daisy, that really hurt me. To me, you just said I'm not doing a good job."

That nearly broke my heart. I wanted to shout at her, "Don't you know I love you? Don't you know who I am? *I'm* the wounded one. I don't hurt people; they hurt me."

That moment made me start wondering who people really saw when they looked at me. I'd kind of expected people would read my heart, even though I kept it guarded and protected and even though I held people at arm's length.

I thought it was their responsibility to see the real me under all my paint.

I could *feel* depression gaining ground. I continued to go to church. I went to prayer meetings every week and joined every ministry you could name. I wanted to find the answer, with all my heart. I prayed, "Lord, tell me what to do, and I will do it." I exercised, ate healthy foods, read my Bible and even asked older women for help. I did everything in my power to fix myself.

And then one day I finally realized that I couldn't.

🦢•🦢•🦢

The bedroom door slammed.

Then the kitchen door downstairs.

I heard Tom drive off and sank onto the bed. It had been a particularly awful argument.

Fine! I don't care.

I screamed into my pillow, unleashing five years of depression into a heart-wrenching sob session and relinquishing the last bit of hope in my heart.

Our marriage was hanging by a thread. We both had too much baggage, and it was suffocating us.

But I don't want a divorce. I'd just marry another man and end up right back here again.

I started thinking of all my options. I couldn't face the idea of becoming a single mom.

Yeah, right. That would sure make Mom happy, wouldn't it?

No, divorce was not an option. Nor was going back to the way things were. Something had to change.

Well, then, I guess that leaves suicide.

Alarm bells clanged in my head. I knew enough to realize that when you start to plan how to kill yourself, that's a huge warning sign. But I stifled the noise and moved forward, deciding how it would play out — park the car in the garage or what?

I had to figure out the least painful way, and the least disturbing, out of consideration for the person who discovered me.

I started to get out of bed; perhaps we had enough sleeping pills in the bathroom.

These days, I believe that the Lord was with me in that moment. I remember pulling the covers off and thinking, *Don't get out of bed. Just don't move.* I felt as if I were being held in my bed — not in a nurturing way, but more like a straight-jacket hug, the way a parent calms a flailing child. Too exhausted to fight it, I lay back down for a long time, just thinking. Eventually, I stopped thinking of myself and thought of my girls. They were still so young. What would happen to them?

I sat up with a bolt.

If I do this, it will hurt them deeply. They will carry resentment, probably for the rest of their lives. This one act could change their direction entirely. Can I really be this selfish?

My mind slowly cleared, and I thought of another option: get help.

I took myself to the hospital the next day and accepted a prescription for antidepressants. Surely, medication would take my burden away.

Life got a little easier. Tom and I agreed to stay together and keep working on our marriage. After a few days, I told Mom about the meds.

"You just don't have enough faith," she said. "If you did, you wouldn't be depressed."

ॐॐॐ

I did it. I defeated my own demons, all by myself. I was once again Not a Victim, only better. Now I had a new story of victory. I was the girl who had been through something hard and pulled herself up and pushed through it.

Or so I thought.

The medication gave me some of my life back. With renewed energy, I tried to resume my role in the church as Super Helper. My pastor asked me if I would consider working with a group that ministered to people in crisis.

"I don't think so," I replied. "I don't want to sit and listen to people's problems."

But I openly shared my own and how I'd overcome them. I shared my story of victory to anyone who would listen, especially Melanie. I wanted her to care about my hurt and understand my needs. I told her constantly. One day, she just rolled her eyes and said, "I know, Mom, I get it. Grandma was mean to you."

The next Sunday at church, I listened to our pastor talking about hurt, and he said, "Hurt makes us who we are."

I knew his parents had been divorced, but my icy heart offered no sympathy.

What does he know about hurt? That was nothing compared to —. Then an idea popped into my head that started a strange sort of two-way conversation.

So, you're saying someone has to be hurt more than you before you will value what he or she says?

My cynicism surprised me, but I thought, *You don't understand how much I hurt.*

What if you gave me your hurts?

I felt like Alice in Wonderland when she fell down the rabbit hole, not just because I realized I was arguing with God, but also because I couldn't quite process the request.

Give it up? No way!

I was afraid to imagine a Daisy without hurts. My story *was* my hurt.

I can't! I won't have anything left! Panic rose, tightening in my throat. *I'm not even a person without my hurt. I would be directionless, out of control.*

It was a turning point for me. For the first time, I was forced to consider the possibility that I still hadn't dealt with my burden and that everyone knew but me.

I didn't want to be *that girl.* I didn't want them to pity me or whisper about me.

"It's too bad about Daisy, she's so broken."

"What a shame. She's been abused, so she needs help."

STRIPPING THE PAINTED HOUSE

No, no! That's not me, I wanted to shout. *I'm tough. I'm a victor, not a victim.*

I continued to search for help and deeper instruction at our church, but counseling programs were not offered there, and I felt at a loss. We began searching for another church.

That's when we found Church on the Rock, a warm, welcoming church with some powerful paint thinner.

᷆᷆᷆᷆

Pastor Bill gave me a friendly smile as I took a seat. I'd been attending Church on the Rock long enough to know I wanted to stay. The people in the congregation had welcomed our family, even before I could tell them what I had to offer. Everywhere I looked I saw a friendly face and open arms.

The pastor began his sermon, and soon I was drawn in to the story of Paul's ministry.

I want to be like Paul, I thought. *He went through so much, like I have, and still he inspired others. I want to affect people the way he did.*

I noticed that, even though I was looking directly at Bill as he preached, I couldn't hear what he was saying. Instead, I was listening to that now-familiar voice that would not be ignored.

Daisy, your bitterness is holding you back.

Bitterness?

I'm not bitter ... am I?

I cannot use you if you're bitter.

The idea of being useless hit me like a slap. Tears began to press against the brim of my eyes and then streamed down my face.

The pastor ended his sermon by telling us about the church's Care for the Heart ministry.

"It's a program that uses prayer and counseling to help you address past hurts and learn how to forgive."

Forgive? I already forgave my stepfather, and my mother doesn't deserve forgiveness. Who else is left?

I processed my thoughts. It was as if there was hope of seeing past the paint to the girl underneath — a girl who couldn't trust adults and who didn't understand what real love was. I didn't really understand. All these unfamiliar words grated like sandpaper against my painted-over self — hurts, bitterness, forgiveness. It made my head spin.

That weekend we went to a friend's home for a multi-family picnic. I watched my youngest girls running around with children their age, but 12-year-old Melanie sat with me on a wooden swing while I chatted with other moms. She'd always done this, and always, when someone spoke to her she'd scoot closer to me. With a start, I realized that I'd taught her this behavior. I knew without asking that she felt like an outsider. She didn't trust and didn't want to be judged, so she hid.

It was another moment of stark clarity. I was teaching my kids what I'd learned: how to protect yourself so that people can't get close to you, how to put up walls, how to judge people, how to be more "right" than other people.

STRIPPING THE PAINTED HOUSE

I don't want her to be like me, I thought. *I don't want her to be — oh my, the Lord was right. I am bitter!*

༁ ༁ ༁

I went to Care for the Heart ministry for help. This was a big step for someone accustomed to being tough. Over a series of meetings, I began to feel loved.

I was surrounded by people who listened without judging and who prayed for and with me with such a tangible outpouring of love that I usually left in a soggy mess of glad tears.

During my time in Care for the Heart, I learned what the real me looked like. One day, as I prayed with some women from the ministry, I saw my hurt from the Lord's perspective. I pictured a balance scale, weighed down with my bag of hurts on one side. It was so heavy the scale tipped to the ground and could not be raised. I knew God was showing me how my hurt had impacted my life.

On the other side of the scale, I envisioned the Lord pouring a sand-like substance from a giant silver scoop and understood it to be his love. The weight of this love flowed over the sides of the scale and lifted all that hurt with ease, and I could breathe. It was as if a ton of bricks had been removed from my chest. At last, I understood. My identity had been formed by circumstances in my life and in all the ways I strived to prove my value. No longer! I started to see that my true identity was in all the Lord had done for me and how much he wanted to love me.

I felt deep peace about letting God love me. He took me back to that little girl who didn't think she could trust adults and helped me relearn what a little girl in a healthy relationship with her father looks like. She trusts. She believes that when she jumps off the stage that her dad is going to catch her. She knows that what he says is true. She runs to him and says, "Help me with this leg that fell off my doll," and knows he will. She knows he has the answers and that he'll pick her up when she's crying and hold her.

Once I learned to trust God with my hurt, then I had to learn to forgive. It wasn't easy; it was a gradual process that required a lot of prayer. Forgiving my mother proved to be the most difficult.

I earnestly wanted to forgive her, but for some reason, I just couldn't. I'd become accustomed to talking with God as I prayed, so it no longer surprised me to find myself thinking both sides of a conversation. One day, as I prayed to be able to release that burden, I just pleaded with him, *Lord, I need you to do it because I can't.*

And I heard the words, *I've got you covered.*

I'd just read a Bible story about a man who owed billions of dollars to his employer, and when he couldn't pay, he begged for mercy, and the employer forgave the debt. Then this man went to someone who owed him only a few hundred dollars and demanded payment. Despite the debtor's pleas for mercy, the man had him thrown in prison.

In my mind, I saw myself making out checks to pay

my debts, using a "forgiveness account," but I was down to $5. I was trying to forgive my mother with insufficient funds, basing my ability to pay on how much I had.

In my view, she had to earn my forgiveness. Because she couldn't, it was a no-win situation, until God covered the tab. His account was overflowing — I knew he was good for it. This allowed me to release the debt I believed she owed me and made forgiveness possible. I still pray that one day she'll find the same peace.

Learning about the Lord's ability and desire to help me was like finding a major puzzle piece and slipping it into place. After eight years, I stopped taking medication for depression. I still feel pain, but it doesn't cripple me. I remember now that there's a solution, and I'm not afraid of it. I'm actually grateful for my depression, realizing it was the Lord's way of stripping away my self-reliance and my attempts to define my identity by deeds or labels.

I found a last major puzzle piece when I realized that I'm not tough, and that's okay. I don't have to be strong. I want to be that little girl who says, "Hey, Dad, can I just crawl up and cuddle in your lap and let you love me?"

My needs didn't make me weak. They made me real. It felt good to be vulnerable because actually it's beautiful when people see who you really are.

After years of watching me learn to be vulnerable, my girls started thriving, unashamed in their love for the Lord, and Melanie was no longer afraid to start a friendship. In fact, she went on mission trips, eager to meet new people. The love I felt for those around me was genuine, and I knew that through my trials the Lord was preparing me to help others who have suffered similar hurts. When people started describing their struggles and saying, "You probably think this isn't a big deal," I could honestly and lovingly say, "No, I get it. You hurt."

Nearly all the paint has been stripped away from my front porch, and my Painter of Truth, Jesus, is laying down some amazingly new and genuinely welcoming colors. I'm still growing and changing, but I get better every day. Even my mother-in-law pulled Tom aside and asked him, "What's up with Daisy? She's changed. She's so joyful and fun to be around, and she seems genuine."

He said he wasn't sure, but I think he's figuring it out. I have a new identity.

God is my daddy, and I'm his beloved daughter.

SLAYING THE DRAGON
THE STORY OF SHAWN AND BETH
WRITTEN BY MELISSA HARDING

Shawn

I had to tell her. But how? What would she say?

"Honey, I have to tell you something." I grabbed Beth's hand and looked into her trusting eyes, trying to steady my racing heart.

"What is it, babe? Whatever it is, we'll get through it." Her voice soothed me, like a gentle embrace. Still, fear slithered down my spine.

I can't do this. I might lose everything. My marriage. My children. Better to keep this where it belongs — in the dark — where it will be safe. She wouldn't stay if she knew.

I looked over at Beth, her beautiful face tight with worry, and my courage sank. *How much was the truth worth? Was it worth losing the life we'd worked so hard to build? Were the lies really hurting anyone?*

I held my face in my hands and sighed.

Could I really risk losing everything?

ल ल ल

I was born to parents who wanted the best for me and did everything they could to make me feel safe and loved. When I was 7, we settled in Ohio, and the years passed with the carefree rhythm of childhood. I attended a Christian school, ranked at the top of my class and had lots of good friends.

In my family and at school, God was a part of daily life. We were taught to follow him and live in a way that pleased him. We learned this meant living contrary to the culture around us. I wanted to go to heaven, and I thought that meant I had to say the right prayer. I worried that if I didn't "say it right," I would spend eternity in the torment of hell. So I repeated this prayer over and over again, hoping that somehow I would get it right.

Overall, life was good, though, and I grew into a young man full of hope for the years ahead. But as I arrived on the cusp of adolescence, my parents delivered some news that jolted me like a slap on the face.

"Son, we're moving to Washington."

"What do you mean?" I gasped. "We can't just move to Washington. All my friends are here in Ohio. You can't make me go."

They did. As we neared the West Coast, driving along a winding, dark gorge, I watched the rain gushing across the road.

How could they bring me to this bleak and dismal place? I had to leave everything behind. How could they do this to me?

I felt small and lost and lonely.

❧❧❧

SLAYING THE DRAGON

My loneliness and feelings of isolation grew as we settled into our new home. Being homeschooled and the new kid in town, I didn't immediately make friends. So when some buddies from Ohio came to visit, I was excited to see them. But one of the boys expressed a sexual curiosity in private that made me feel confused, ashamed and dirty. That marked the end of our friendship, and of any desire I had to return to Ohio, and marked the beginning of a deep, secret sense of shame and disgust.

One day not long after, on the side of the road, I found a discarded magazine full of explicit images. What started as an innocent bike ride that day led to the discovery of a path into a fantasy world of self-gratification. I pored over the photographs, and they came to fill my imagination.

On the outside, I remained a rule following model of perfection. But in my mind, I escaped to a world where I was a king and conqueror, surrounded by unclothed beauties.

We joined a home school co-op, and I played the role expected of me. I wore the right clothes, said the right words and obeyed the rules.

I learned that if I behaved well, God would reward me. If I messed up, though, I deserved to be punished.

Sexual purity was one of the greatest measures of good behavior, we were told, and we should control our desires because sex was meant for marriage and self-gratification was not acceptable. God might strike dead anyone who participated in self-gratification, as he supposedly did in the Bible.

But I was regularly having impure thoughts, and God didn't strike me dead. *What did that mean? Did the grownups instructing us really have the answers? Or were they as confused as I was?*

The rules seemed clear, but deep down I wondered how I could ever measure up to such high expectations. *How did other people not make wrong choices?* But nobody around me seemed to be wondering about these questions, so I stuffed my secrets further down inside where no one could ever discover them.

෴෴෴

Beth

I sat at the kitchen table, watching Shawn's face. His hands shook as he held my hand. He looked up at me, and I saw the fear in his eyes.

Oh, no. What is going on? What could he possibly need to tell me that is making him this afraid? I couldn't imagine.

Shawn was the man of my dreams. A man who worked hard for our family, Shawn was everything I'd ever wanted in a husband. I was living my fairytale, with two kids, a house on 5 acres and a bright future ahead of us. The road hadn't been easy, for sure. But together we could get through anything.

Couldn't we?

෴෴෴

SLAYING THE DRAGON

I grew up on a farm, in a safe and loving family, and spent my childhood caring for our animals, growing food in the garden and roaming the land. My five siblings and I were homeschooled, and our parents poured their life's wisdom into us. I learned at an early age that God was good, and he had good things in store for us if we followed his ways. I was a good girl, and my heart yearned to follow God. My childish conclusion rendered faith into a sort of equation: I would work for God, and he would work for me. As I looked toward the future, I anticipated a life full of hope and promise.

"Come on, Beth. It'll make me happy. Don't you want me to be happy? If you won't help me, I will kill myself." Of course I wanted my cousin to be happy. I wanted everyone to be happy. I felt a deep love for people, and at times the burden to please them buried me under its weight. Dazed by the attention of my 18-year-old cousin, I tried to tell him what I believed to be true about God and his love for us. It didn't help. That's not what my cousin wanted. It wasn't ever what he wanted from me.

I ran to the woods, the place I felt most alive. Surrounded by the comfort of the trees, I let my tears run free. I could still feel my cousin's kiss burning on my lips. And couldn't shake the feeling of guilt. It felt good to be noticed, but had I led him on in some way? Were my parents right? Was I a flirt? Was I responsible for provoking his behavior? I didn't intend to lead him on. No matter how good I tried to be, I always seemed to get in my own way.

"Oh, God! What's wrong with me? I want to serve you. I want to do the things that please you. But this doesn't make sense! Nobody understands!"

From deep within me, I heard a gentle voice: *My beautiful child. I'm here. I see you, and I love you. Trust me. Look to me. I am all that you need.*

❧❧❧

Shawn

I sat in the church pew, listening to the pastor speak and deeply aware of my hidden guilt. Looking around at the people I knew, I wondered whether any of them kept secrets, too. I knew how to pretend everything was okay while hiding my shame.

To the world, I was the charming gentleman any parent hoped for their daughter to find. I sang with church groups, traveled internationally with a worship team, went on a foreign mission trip and mentored young men in the Bible.

No one knew about my private fantasies or the time I spent looking at explicit magazines and X-rated movies. I knew it was wrong, but the more I told myself to stop, the stronger the pull became.

You're the only one who struggles with this. Look at all of them. They wouldn't understand. They are perfect. Look at you. You're a sorry excuse for a man.

I berated myself, but lust overpowered my resolve to resist it.

"God, help me!" I cried out time and time again. I read the Bible. I prayed.

Then returned to the tantalizing world of pornography and its temporary thrill and satisfaction.

Beneath my pious disguise, I privately doubted God. *If he wasn't going to take away the temptation, then why should I bother? Why keep trying to meet strict moral standards if God wasn't going to do his part? After all, he made me this way, right?* I lacked the vision or the skills to fight my sexual urges. By this time, I'd also lost the will.

Rather than permitting dating, my parents encouraged courting. This meant only pursuing someone I intended to marry. All physical affection should be saved until the wedding night, my "ticket to freedom." The lust in my heart could finally be satisfied in an acceptable way once I got married.

I found a girl to court and started counting down the time until I could consummate the relationship. She was much younger than me, though. It would be years before we could marry. I wanted to do the right thing, but lust controlled my thoughts and desires, and I did its bidding.

I can't do this anymore. She deserved better than this — better than me. Although everyone perceived me to be an honorable man, I knew my intentions were anything but honorable. I only wanted one thing from her, and the wait was more than I could stand.

"How could you do this to us?!" Her parents couldn't believe that the guy who had promised his future to their daughter was throwing it all away.

Little did they know I was throwing away more than just a courtship. After years of trying, after begging for a miracle, God hadn't answered my prayers. At 23, I didn't care anymore.

Maybe God doesn't really care what I am going through down here. I'm trying, I really am, it's just not working.

Shortly after, I met a girl and pursued her and a reckless, short-lived relationship. *Why keep fighting a battle I was never going to win?*

I gave up the fight and my virginity.

ஃஃஃ

Beth

I stood at the register in the local drugstore. As I went to pay, I saw him. Our eyes locked, and my heart skipped 10 beats. I couldn't believe my eyes. Six years earlier, at age 12, I'd heard him sing at a friend's funeral. Not only was he the most handsome man I'd ever seen, but his voice and confidence took my breath away. I'd told myself that he was the man I wanted to marry. And here he was, standing across the drugstore from me. He smiled, and I smiled back. The room spun, and my heart beat against my chest like a wild horse trying to escape. I bee-lined it out of the store, afraid that if I stayed I would flirt. I wanted so desperately to be the good girl I knew I should be. I hurried out to my car and rushed home. I didn't trust myself around guys. The temptation to get their attention and affection weakened my resolve every time. *God, what is happening? What did that mean? I want to pursue YOU with all my heart. I don't want to flirt or chase after guys. Help!*

But I couldn't shake the image of his face. I found my mind replaying the whole encounter and felt perplexed by my emotions. I couldn't ignore the butterflies swarming in my stomach at the thought of his eyes looking into mine. *Okay, God. If this is something from you, then let me see him again in the next week.*

Two days later, I wandered through a video store, waiting for my little brother to pick a movie, when I felt a wave of heat wash over me. The hair on my arms tingled, and I looked up to see HIM! It was the guy from the other day! I fumbled my way through the store, confused and excited by my attraction to this man. When I arrived at my car, I found a business card on my windshield. Catching my breath, I looked at it and saw Shawn's name and number written on it. I knew I would call, but I promised God that if Shawn didn't follow him, I would hang up the phone. Well, Shawn did follow God and with all his heart!

From our first date, we were best friends. We shared so much in common and quickly fell madly in love. We led worship at church together, studied the Bible together and spent every possible minute together. I wanted to save myself for marriage, and Shawn said he did as well. He told me I was his first kiss, and I believed him. Our passion for each other grew stronger as the months passed, and we anticipated the day both our hearts and bodies would become one.

As our passion blazed, the lines of purity blurred. I had strong boundaries, but I didn't understand why the things Shawn thought were okay felt so wrong. I loved this man! He was a good man who loved God. He was a leader in our church, and he loved me. He wouldn't push me to do something that was wrong, would he? We didn't know what purity looked like in a relationship, so I pushed aside my concerns and gave in to the pressure of his affection. Something didn't feel right, didn't feel pure, but maybe it was just me.

かかか

The mountains of Sweden towered over us as we gazed across the landscape. The lights of the town twinkled, their reflection in the water winking at us as if they held secrets we would never know. Shawn held me in his strong arms, and I breathed in the wonder and beauty surrounding us.

"I love you, Beth!" Shawn shouted across the water. I laughed, resting my head against his solid chest.

Suddenly, he dropped to one knee, took my hands and said, "Beth, you're the girl I waited my whole life to find. You're the girl I prayed for. I love you, and I want to spend the rest of my life with you. Will you marry me?"

I gasped, tears pouring down my cheeks. We held each other, crying and praying. I didn't want to ever let him go.

He looked deep into my eyes with a love so entrancing,

it seemed as if time stood still. He wiped the tears from my face, trailing his fingers down my cheeks. "Does that mean you'll marry me?"

I laughed, cupped his face in my hands and whispered, "Yes. Of course I'll marry you!"

In June of 1997, we pledged our lives to each other before hundreds of friends and family. Our hearts melded into one as we built a home on 5 acres.

God had rewarded me with an incredible husband, and I gazed into my bright, promising future with thankfulness and expectation.

⾾⾾⾾

Shawn

"I'm sorry, Mr. and Mrs. Brighton. I have some bad news." The doctor looked up from his papers, and when I saw the look of sympathy on his face, my heart plummeted into my stomach.

"You're not carrying a baby after all. What you have is a tumor that is making your body think it's pregnant. You have all the hormones of a normal pregnancy, but there isn't a baby."

"What does this mean?" I asked, but I didn't want to know the answer.

"Well, I'm afraid the blood tests show that the tumor is cancerous. We need to perform an emergency DNC, to prevent further life-threatening bleeding and start chemo treatments immediately."

RESCUE

I watched my beautiful bride fight for her life over the next several months. The chemotherapy tore her body apart, and I stood helplessly by her side. Our firstborn son, Andrew, was just a toddler, and the thought of him losing his mother was more than I could bear.

This is my punishment, I determined. God was punishing me, and I had to admit, I deserved it. While I had turned my back on God for a time, I came back, desperate for his presence in my life. The moment I saw Beth in the video store, I knew she was the one for me. She was the whole package — beautiful, kind and pure! *Why had I not waited for her? Why had I given up hope?* I pursued her heart even while my mind pursued her flesh. I thought that getting married would take away my desire to retreat to my fantasies, but it didn't. In fact, as the years went by, I sank deeper and deeper into the pit of sexual impurity, sneaking away on business trips to strip clubs and finally introducing Beth to X-rated movies. My lust was like a dragon chained to my leg, one I couldn't get away from. The cravings compelled me to keep looking, keep wanting. I tried to escape, but my resolve never lasted long. If I starved the dragon, it would roar in hunger, breathing fire down my neck. I could fight fires that raged in other people's homes, but I couldn't put out this fire in my mind. It took my mind away from our home, our property, our dreams, and it burned constantly, begging for my attention. I discovered if I fed it just a little bit at a time, I could keep the dragon satisfied.

As I watched Beth fight for her life, the dragon raged

out of control. I was a successful firefighter, a respected leader in our church and a loving father and husband. But no one knew what lurked beneath my well-crafted façade. And no one would ever find out.

ৡৡৡ

Beth

My insides lurched as I tried to stand up. *I have to get out of this bed!* No amount of determination would make my body do what I wanted. I lay back down, unable to fight the battle raging within me. The chemo brought my fever up to toxic levels, and my once-healthy body was now riddled with sickness. Feelings of worthlessness consumed me. *How could I serve God trapped in this bed? How could I be a mother to my 1-year-old son?* My husband needed me. My church needed me. Didn't God need me? I begged God to help, but he was silent. *What did I do to deserve this?!* I had worked so hard for God. *How could something like this happen to me? I thought good things happen to good people! Had I not pleased God with my life? WHY?*

"Where are you, God?" I cried with the little strength I had left. "I've done everything you asked. I've made the right choices. I've served you with all my heart. Where are you when I need you? What am I supposed to do?"

Nothing. I heard nothing. *Maybe God didn't exist. And if he did, he must be someone very different from the God I had served my whole life.*

"If you're there, God, you're going to have to show me! I can't see you, and I can't feel you. If you care at all, show me!"

I surrendered to the painful loneliness in my heart, feeling separated from God. He had been there for me so many times in the past. *Why did it feel like he'd turned his back to me?* The next day, I was going in for another chemo treatment. There was a chance they would need to do a hysterectomy, threatening my dreams of having a big family. My exhausted heart felt hopeless. *What would tomorrow hold?*

I went to sleep feeling numb.

The next morning, sunlight danced across the windowpane, and I opened my eyes and smiled. Like ice melting in the warmth of the sun, I could feel the light breaking through the hard shell around my heart.

"God, is that you? What do you want me to do?"

The same voice I came to know so well over the years whispered to my soul. It was as if he said, *My child, I don't want you to do anything. You don't have to perform for me. I love you because you are mine, not because of anything you can do for me. Be still, and let me carry you through this time. Let me show my power in your life.*

Joy and peace bubbled up within me. *Was it possible? Did God really love me simply because I was his daughter and not because of all the good things I did to try to please him?* As a child, my parents taught me that nothing I did could earn my way to heaven. Jesus came to earth and died to save me from the bad things in my heart that separated me from God. I knew I didn't need to work to get to heaven. But work to earn God's favor in my life? That was ingrained in me from the time I learned to talk. Good things happen to good people, right?

I realized that morning how much God loved me. I didn't have to perform for him. Bad things happen, even to good people. God is still good. Singing, speaking and leading were gifts God gave me, but they didn't make him love me more. A new passion rose up within me to get to know this God who loved me even when I was too weak to serve him. I wanted to follow him, not for the rewards he would give me, but simply to know his heart and delight in his affection for me.

That morning, I went to the doctor, unafraid of what the prognosis would be.

"Can you check my blood levels before we do the treatment?" Something within me nudged me to ask the doctor. Peace washed over me as we waited for the results. Whatever the future held, I felt I was safe in the arms of God.

"Well, it's a miracle!" The doctor stared at the paper in disbelief. "The cancer counts are down!"

Shawn and I welled up with joy. My body was saved from the extra load of medicine, and I wouldn't need the hysterectomy!

After a year of mandatory birth control, cancer remission and the hard work of regaining my health, I was amazed to find myself pregnant again. I rejoiced and praised God. When Max was born, I ran my fingers over his soft skin, and my heart overflowed with thankfulness. I recognized that my gratefulness was deeper after my fight with cancer, when I learned not to take my health or many blessings for granted. I could not have been happier!

ନ୍ତନ୍ତନ୍ତ

Shawn

No, I can't do it. I can't tell anyone. I'll lose everything.

The dragon seethed. Although Beth's body gained strength every day, things were far from okay. She knew something wasn't right. I tried to pressure her into going on an X-rated retreat, and for the first time she said no to something I'd tried to convince her to do. Before, she'd always followed my insistent lead. She was changing, though. She saw what fantasy was doing to our marriage. I grew tired of the lies and exhausted from the duplicity. *Would I ever be free of this beast?* I longed to be the man everyone thought I was, but I just couldn't risk telling the people I loved the truth.

Over the years, I not only told lies to protect myself, I believed the lie that, by lying, I was protecting my wife. *After all, it was only hurting me, right? My actions didn't hurt anyone else. What my wife didn't know wouldn't hurt her.*

Whenever the truth tried to claw its way out, the lies rushed to stop it. *You won't be respected if you tell someone, but you're respected now, so keep it a secret. People look up to you. Your wife adores you. You're the one paying the consequences. If no one knows, then no one gets hurt.*

A friend from work who also went to our church began to open up about his struggles with pornography. His marriage began to fall apart, and like emergency responders rushing to the scene of an accident, we dashed to their sides to offer assistance. While ignoring my own struggles and arrogantly assuming I had things under control, I began reading a book called *Restoring the Fallen* in an attempt to help my friend. As I read, though, the words spoke to my conscience.

At first I resisted the book's wisdom. The author insisted that truth and solid mentorship was the key to freedom. I didn't want that to be the key. I wanted freedom, of course, but not through truth and having to share my struggle with others. As the days passed, though, I couldn't keep running. I knew what I needed to do, but my courage wilted with fear.

I wrestled with God. *Don't make me tell her! I'll lose her. I'll lose everything.*

For my entire life, I'd tried to be the person I thought I should be and who I really wanted to be. And on the outside, I succeeded. But the turmoil inside ate me apart. *How much did I really want to change? What was I willing to lose?* Suddenly, a light turned on.

"Forgive me, God. I don't want to live like this anymore."

And then I heard God speak through a verse in the Bible I knew by heart. *Shawn, the truth will set you free.*

God's forgiveness and love washed over me. For as long as I could remember, I tried to fight the dragon of lust on my own, and while I experienced periods of relief, the chains never broke. Every time I had tried to change, my efforts were not enough. I tried everything I knew — abstaining from food, praying, begging God to take it away. But these provided only short-lived control before I would lose even more ground and slip deeper into my secrecy and shame.

The book helped me realize that God wanted me to do something different. He wanted my honesty. I had to open up myself before him, with all my flaws, so that he could reach in and heal my wounds. I also needed to tell Beth. It was time.

❧❧❧

"Honey, I have to tell you something." *God, give me strength. I can't do this without you!*

"What is it, babe? I can see you are struggling. Just tell me. We'll get through it together."

I told her everything. How I was drawn again and again to images on the computer and TV. I told her about the strip clubs, the constant urge to fill my mind with images of other women and the fantasy world I brought into our marriage. I poured out the secrets, lies and longings I harbored for so long. This process was like peeling back an onion; it was layers deep, and I'd been so good at guarding my secrets that it was hard, even in the times of opening up, to be completely honest. I rationalized holding back a few pieces of information I thought would be too painful for her to hear.

At first, Beth showed empathy. Her response surprised me and brought me tremendous relief, and her focus on God's desire to bring healing encouraged me to continue to be honest.

As her shock wore off, Beth also began to express how my choices had affected her. It helped me see how my choices had not just hurt me, but they deeply wounded her. She no longer trusted me. She didn't know what was truth or a lie. Her anger and grief came in waves. It was excruciating for both of us.

"I don't know who you are. I don't know anything about you. You've been lying to me for our entire marriage. This is going to take some time to figure out."

It did take time. More time than either of us wanted it to. We showed up at our first counseling appointment, confident that our love was strong enough to overcome anything.

"So, doc," I asked the counselor. "How long do you think this is going to take? How long before things are back to normal?"

He looked at me, his eyes soft with compassion. "Well, Shawn, how long have you been lying to your wife?"

"Seven years."

"Then it will take at least that long."

We left his office, hand in hand, laughing at his naivety. *He obviously doesn't know who we are. We are the worship leaders, prayer warriors, Bible study leaders. We would be back to normal in no time.*

We were not seeing clearly. It was like we wanted new glasses but had the wrong prescription. Things were blurry.

While we believed it was important to confide in people we trusted, sometimes doing so left us more confused. Some people called it a shame and said we made God look bad by being honest about our failures. Others blamed Beth and said she should realize all guys behave like this and just get over it.

ॐॐॐ

Fireworks blasted outside our window, their bright lights sizzling against the black sky. Beth and I lay in bed. She breathed softly, while my mind wrestled with whether I should confess to her the one remaining secret. In an effort to protect her, I hadn't revealed the whole truth. But if it wasn't that big of a deal, why couldn't I shake it from my mind?

The truth will set you free. The words haunted me, following me through my days like a shadow. I wasn't free. Not yet.

Please, God. I don't want to tell her.

As the fireworks reminded me of our nation's independence, I faced the question I had been running from for so long.

How much is your freedom worth, Shawn? You say you want to be freed from this dragon, but are you willing to do whatever it takes? Yes, you might lose this beautiful life you've built, but in the end, will your freedom be worth it?

Okay, God. If you want me to tell her, I will. But I need to know for sure. Have her turn over to me and ask me.

Within minutes, Beth turned and faced me. "Shawn, what do you need to tell me?"

Emotions of shock and relief hit me. God wanted me to be completely free! I felt his presence, like a hand encouraging me forward.

"I didn't want you to know because I thought it would hurt you too much." I took a deep breath, and as the tears fell, I admitted what I'd planned never to tell her. "I told you that you were the first girl I ever kissed. I lied, Beth. I wasn't even a virgin when I met you."

"Oh, Shawn." She sighed with compassion. "Somehow I knew you had this weight on you. I'm so sorry. Thank you for loving me so much that you were honest with me."

"I wanted to be the man you deserved. I wanted you — I wanted everyone — to think I was really the perfect guy I appeared to be. I told myself that you would never love me if you knew the truth."

"But, Shawn, I do love you! More than anything, I want to know you, the REAL YOU! Don't ever stop being honest. I know God will show us the way. I just know it."

With joy and deep emotion, I whispered, "Tonight, I'm free. It's my Independence Day. Freedom from the lies and deception. It feels so good that you finally know who I really am. I'm so sorry, Beth."

Her strength blew me away, and I wanted nothing more than to prove to her that I was truly ready to change. We cried together, believing that as much as we loved each other, only God could do the impossible in our marriage. It wasn't Shawn or Beth who would swoop in and save the day.

"I can't stay married to a man who fills his heart and mind with impurity and dishonesty," Beth informed me. "I want you to choose what God's word says to do. The habits we have must be reprogrammed with new, healthy habits. This could be the 'long road' our counselor was telling us about. I want to go back there. I think we need to stop thinking we have all the answers, because we don't. I want the tools needed to fight this battle and win. I want the best God has for us, Shawn. If you really want to change, and you're willing to do whatever it takes, then I am here. I will fight this battle with you."

ॐॐॐ

Beth

After Shawn's "Independence Day," we faced many hard, hopeless days. I couldn't believe that I married a man who could lie to me for so many years. I walked through every stage of grief imaginable. Sometimes simply getting out of bed meant a successful day. Well-meaning friends offered advice and support, but many simply wanted to place a Band-Aid on our pain. We weren't interested in a Band-Aid. We wanted total and complete healing. Just like a soldier wounded in battle needs intensive care, we knew that this was more than just a superficial injury. We were wounded in the battle for our hearts and minds. We needed a miracle to bring our lives back to the way God had intended. There wasn't a magic button we could press to make it better. Shawn and I tried fixing the part on the outside, but it never set us free on the inside. Honesty and transparency, lots of prayer and solid mentorship were the keys to our freedom.

As I searched through my memories, it became so clear to me how God had actually answered the prayers I'd had as a little girl. I had always wanted to have a marriage that spoke of God's presence and guidance. Little did I know how that prayer would be answered through a difficult and painful journey.

In those hard times, God's word came alive to us.

People prayed for God to pour love and hope into our hearts and minds. We found several godly mentors who had faced and overcome the same challenges. It was humbling and incredible to learn from them. Our lifestyle drastically changed. At first, it was hard. As the months turned into years, the changes we made brought us to a place of appreciation for what was beautiful, good and healthy for us. I fell in love all over again, with a man I respected more than ever before. We learned what it meant to celebrate our love with clean hearts and minds.

᙮᙮᙮

Shawn

Restoring broken trust was difficult.

At the encouragement of counselors, I decided to take a polygraph to prove my truthfulness. After passing two polygraphs, I reestablished trust with Beth.

I realized, through counseling, that I had to starve the dragon in order to break its hold on my mind. It meant hard work, but I wasn't alone anymore. I allowed God's presence in every moment of the day. We found people who understood the anguish and joy of our journey, who walked with us all along the way. And I had Beth, fighting with me, reminding me to never give up.

The movies we watched, the places we chose to go and the decisions we made all became part of the battle. We woke up each morning ready to fight, unwilling to allow the dragon one more piece of our lives. The stakes were too great to ignore. We needed each other in this battle. Arms linked and shields raised, we could move forward together in victory.

Ten years ago, I came clean with my life choices. It felt so good to be free of the lust, the lies, the hiding — fully known and fully loved. I learned to live transparently and honestly with all around me. No more pretending, no more acting. God healed my heart, the brokenness inside. I learned to see the battle clearly, and I learned the way to fight back. The long, difficult work to repair my marriage was absolutely worth it.

Our relationship showed what God can do. I gained a new appreciation and admiration for Beth. I savored our friendship with a healed heart, keeping my eyes for her alone. I believed it's what God always desired for me, and I finally saw how awesome, fulfilling and satisfying true intimacy could be.

అలా

Beth

Shawn stepped toward me and I saw him as a warrior, a dragon slayer. I had never been more in love with him. Not because he was perfect, but because I knew him — all of him. He took my hand. I thought about the days when I wasn't sure we'd find our way. But the more I got to know God, the more I realized how vast his love was for us. We didn't have to perform for him. We didn't have to work to experience his goodness. He loved us simply because we were his, and that was enough.

I breathed in, drinking in the love surrounding us. Shawn looked at me, and I melted in the glow of his love, just like I did that first day our eyes met. Hand in hand, we stepped forward, ready to face our future together.

A DOSE OF HOPE
THE STORY OF JOHN
WRITTEN BY LISA BRADSHAW

When we arrived at the emergency room, I was high from the last line of cocaine I'd snorted before the intervention.

"Watch this, Mom," I said as I breathed in deep. I'd been on a seven-day bender, and I smiled as I inhaled what little cocaine remained inside my nostrils.

"John, what are you doing?" my mom asked in horror.

"Just watch," I said again, this time pointing to the monitor above my bed that was tracking my heart rate.

Within a few seconds, my heart began to race and increased by at least 10 to 15 beats per minute.

"John!"

"Don't worry. Just watch. I know what I'm doing." I started controlling my breathing by taking deep breaths and sitting very still as I watched the monitor detect my heart rate slow dramatically.

"See. Nothing to worry about."

My mom's eyes welled up with tears. She did not say a word but looked at me like she no longer knew the person I'd become. It was obvious she knew I'd sunk to some serious depths in my addiction, depths she did not even want to imagine.

ও ও ও

I heard the glass hit the kitchen floor and shatter.

"D*** it," my mom said quietly to herself with frustration.

I knew she was drunk, so I walked into the kitchen from my bedroom to help her clean up the mess.

"Stay out, John. I've got it," she told me, her words slurred.

My mom had stepped in the broken glass and cut both her feet and was on her hands and knees picking up glass and wiping up the trail of blood that followed her in circles.

"Mom, you're bleeding," I told her, walking toward the one area of the kitchen not covered in glass and her blood. "Let me help you."

"I've got it," my dad interjected as he entered the kitchen. "It's late. You've got school tomorrow. Go get ready for bed."

My dad grabbed two kitchen towels and wrapped them tightly around my mom's feet to help stop the bleeding, then walked her to a chair.

I reluctantly did as my dad asked, left the room and started getting ready for bed.

సౌసౌసౌ

My mom wrecked three cars, got a few DUIs and smashed a few windows while intoxicated. My dad's role was to clean up any mess while I, as the oldest of five kids, looked out for my younger siblings.

A DOSE OF HOPE

My family moved to Alaska when I was 9 years old. My mom's drinking got worse, and my parents even split up for a few months. All of us kids remained living with my dad, and my mom eventually came back home. We soon returned to the Pacific Northwest to start over again.

I tried drinking as a teenager, but I did not like it at first because the hard alcohol burned my throat. I wanted *something* to help ease my troubles at home and found pot a lot smoother going in. By the summer I was 14, I was hooked on pot. I loved the escape from reality and the happy high it gave me.

As much as I loved it, I did not have much money, and I did not receive an allowance. I decided that the only way to support my newfound pastime was to start selling. The more pot I sold, the more I could afford to smoke.

I'll never do hard drugs or anything more than pot, I told myself.

I mostly sold to people at school, but occasionally people would stop by the house for a few minutes to pick up what they needed, and my phone rang constantly. By the time I was 17, I was one of the main pot dealers at the high school.

"John, get in here," my dad called to me from inside the house.

I'd made part of the garage into my bedroom after telling my parents I wanted some privacy from my younger siblings. It made it easier to deal with the people stopping by at all hours of the night.

"Yeah, Dad?"

"What the h*** are you doing out there? I can smell it upstairs."

The familiar scent of pot made its way through the vents of the house and wafted into my parents' room. By the time my dad found us in a cloud of smoke in the garage, we couldn't hide what we'd been doing.

"Sorry, Dad."

"You better be. Tell everyone to go home. Party's over."

I never got myself in trouble with the law when dealing pot. There were so many near misses, it's still hard to believe I did not go to jail over it. Before I was 18, I got pulled over 12 times. Even when the cops must have smelled pot smoke in the car, I only got a firm warning. Only one time did the cops contact my dad.

"Sir, we'd like you to come to the station to retrieve your son's backpack. He left it behind in his car when it broke down last night," one officer said when leaving a message for my dad. My car had broken down on the side of the road, and I was careless enough to leave my backpack full of pot in the car.

"Son, you're lucky they're willing to just give you a warning," my dad informed me after talking it over with the cops and picking up my bag. "You know you're headed down a bad path." My dad was concerned about the choices I was making. He told me stories about when he was young and used to deal drugs. He tried to scare me away from it, but it didn't work.

It was a close call, but by then, I was hooked, and there

was no way a simple warning was going to stop me from smoking pot. The only way I could afford to keep up with my habit was to sell it.

At school, I cut class every other day and nearly gave up entirely. I barely graduated.

I had no interest in cleaning up. I smoked pot every day, several times a day, because both pot and alcohol helped me escape while helping me feel more bold and outgoing. I was insecure without one or the other. And I hung out with friends who liked doing what I was doing. I went to parties and was surrounded by people who drank and did drugs and had sex in bedrooms with people they barely knew.

I sold the good pot, making me the guy everyone wanted to be around. Dealing helped me go from being invisible to being a cool kid.

As much as I loved smoking pot, after a while I realized it wasn't enough. I was on my way to much bigger highs and much lower lows.

ॐॐॐ

"Dude, you're going to love this," my buddy Scott told me as he lined up the cocaine on a mirror with a razor blade. "Seriously, there's no feeling like it."

He was right. I snorted the entire line, and within seconds, I was overwhelmed with a feeling of pleasure that I had never experienced before.

"Wow. This is incredible," I said as I leaned back on the couch and closed my eyes.

"I told you."

I felt like I was on top of the world. I felt powerful. Any inhibitions and insecurities pot and alcohol failed to tackle, cocaine obliterated from the moment the high came over me. It was a whole new level of high and pleasure.

"I'm going to learn everything I can about this stuff," I told Scott. "Seriously, I'm going to make this my life."

I was instantly hooked on cocaine but bummed when I realized how quickly the high was over. Thirty minutes to an hour didn't seem nearly long enough. The more I consumed, the more I wanted. I knew coke was more expensive than pot, so I began mapping out a way of supporting my drug habit. Soon I was obsessed. Cocaine was the big time, and I knew I had to step up my dealing game if I wanted to keep myself supplied with it.

The friends I partied with in high school were not into hard drugs, so I began distancing myself from them and started seeking out the people in town who were using and dealing cocaine.

I had moved out after I barely graduated high school, and I worked for my dad's business full time, but I soon had a successful business on the side dealing cocaine. As my habit grew, I learned about a guy who lived about an hour away who could get me cocaine in larger quantities.

"Wait till you meet this guy. You'll have plenty of blow from now on," my buddy Ronnie said as he sped down the freeway in his Ford Mustang 5.0. "Get a line ready for me."

We were getting to our meeting with the big-time cocaine dealer in a hurry.

Ronnie handed me the cocaine we'd brought in the car and a CD case for me to cut it on.

"Lean in," I told him as I held up the line I prepared for him as he drove.

Ronnie was already drunk and had been smoking pot before we even got in the car. "Another one," he said as he finished the first line and got ready for the next.

"Stay in your lane, man!" I hollered over the blaring music when he swerved out of our lane and into the next.

"Keep it comin'," he insisted as he corrected and returned to his lane.

Somehow we made it alive to meet with my potential new supplier.

"You a cop?" he asked me as soon as I walked in the house.

"No."

"Cause if you are, this is entrapment," he told me, looking me straight in the eye.

"Seriously, I'm not a cop."

I should have been scared by what I saw and what I was about to do. I should have winced at the sight of a man shooting up heroine on a nearby bed, but I did not see myself as being like him. *I'm definitely not a drug addict,* I thought. *I don't put needles in my arms like these guys.* All I cared about was getting high every second of the day. As long as I stuck to my methods of getting high, I figured I would be fine.

RESCUE

❧ ❧ ❧

My roommate, Justin, also did drugs, but he and his friends were into meth, and he wasn't dealing. By this time, I had a $400-a-day habit, and cocaine ruled my life. It was not uncommon for me to make $1,000 a night. I snorted lines through hundred dollar bills and then just left the bills lying around when I was done.

I felt on top of the world and happier than I'd ever been in my life. I had more money than I ever dreamed of having. I was hooking up with beautiful girls. But as sexy as I thought cocaine was when I started using it, it was only fun for the first few weeks. Before long, I no longer wanted to party and have a good time with my friends and girlfriends. The only thing I wanted to do was get high on coke. I rarely smiled and walked around checking my windows and the peephole in my apartment. When the paranoia set in, I turned off the music and sent the girls away. It was just me and a few friends who liked cocaine as much as I did. We sat in my room and did nothing but cocaine. We did not talk or interact for the most part. Instead we just got high and waited for our turn to hit the pipe or snort a line.

"Shhhh," I would whisper. "Listen. Did you hear that?"

"Hear what?"

"Someone's out there."

"Out where?"

"In the living room. Someone is walking around out there."

"It's probably just Justin. Stop being paranoid."

I was not the most fun guy in the room. I *was* paranoid. I thought people were breaking into my apartment and spying on me.

"Quit stomping your feet like that. Take off your shoes," I demanded. "You're being too loud."

"Dude, I don't even have shoes on. I'm not making any noise."

People who tolerated partying with me knew that they had to tread lightly. The common sound of a car door shutting in our apartment parking lot sounded to me like a team of police slamming their car doors on their way to bust me.

"Who is it? Who is it?" I would ask every time someone's cell phone rang.

"Chill. It's just my girl."

One night, after staring out my window until about 4 a.m., I was convinced the police were outside my apartment, preparing to break in at dawn. I moved all my furniture from the living room and barricaded it against the front door. I thought if they kicked the door in, it would give me more time to run to the bathroom and flush my cocaine down the toilet.

A few weeks later, I locked myself in my bathroom because I thought I heard police in my apartment. My heart pounded so hard I felt like it was going to jump out of my chest. I was covered in sweat and spent hours in that bathroom doing massive amounts of cocaine because I thought it was going to get confiscated, anyway. I did a line, then I held my rock of cocaine over the toilet, ready to drop and flush it at the first sign of the door opening.

When the paranoia became too much and having too many people around was getting to me, I told my roommate and most of my drug buddies that I was moving home to live with my parents. But I did not move back home. I moved into the one-bedroom apartment across the parking lot, so I could be alone with the drugs.

I stopped eating. I stopped having sex. Everything about cocaine that first heightened my senses had ended up reducing me to a gaunt, malnourished, sleep-deprived drug addict waiting on his next fix.

෫෫෫

I'd always said the same prayer every night.

Now I lay me down to sleep, I pray the Lord my soul to keep. If I should die before I wake, I pray the Lord my soul to take.

My parents frequented church and took us kids until I was about 8 years old. About that time, Mom's drinking escalated, my parents fought more and we stopped going to church. I remember being curious about God and interested in learning more about him, but my relationship with God faded to the backdrop of our chaotic lives.

Even though I did not have a personal relationship with him, I had an awareness of him, but I was always running from God. I didn't want to think about him while living as an addict. And finally I got tired of wrestling with my conscience, so I turned it off to see how far letting go would take me.

As a drug dealer, I never used cocaine to get women to sleep with me the way many other men did, and I never mixed the cocaine with baking soda to rip off buyers. I had rules about just how low I would go when dealing drugs and somehow justified my behavior. As a cocaine addict, my drug use escalated to a whole new level when I told God I was setting him aside.

The few people I kept around started worrying about me. I pushed cocaine to the limit every time. If my nose bled from snorting too much, I smoked it. If my left thumb was burned from the lighter, I used my right thumb. When I overdosed, my heart rate increased, my blood pressure took drastic dips and my nose bled for hours.

Scott, the friend who introduced me to cocaine, was the only friend I had left from high school who liked using cocaine the way I used it — constantly and in abundance. Even he was starting to worry about me.

"I think John is in big trouble," he told my mom and dad one night. "He's planning to skip town in the morning and isn't looking good."

The three of them staged an intervention and showed up at my apartment with a friend of my mom's from AA. Scott was high throughout the entire ordeal, and the guy from AA ended up calling his sponsor and leaving. He saw my stash of cocaine and freaked out at the sight of drugs for the first time after he had gotten clean.

"You need to get to the emergency room," my mom told me.

"We'll take you now. Leave all the drugs here," my dad agreed.

I went, but only because I thought it would save me from going to jail. I was certain the cops were zeroing in on me and my entire operation, and I was afraid I was about to get busted.

"You need help. You've gone too far," my dad told me.

"I'm so worried about you, son," my mom cried.

"Okay, let's go," I told them as I grabbed booze from the freezer before walking out the door.

To my mom's horror, I snorted the residual cocaine from my last high while she watched near my hospital bed. The high only lasted for a few minutes. As I came down, I felt overwhelmed by my decision to go with my parents.

"Get me out of here!" I yelled, trying to rip the IV from my arm and get out of the hospital bed.

"Don't move!" my dad shouted as he forced my arms down, holding me still for as long as he could.

My mom stood frozen in the corner of the hospital room.

"No! No!" I continued to shout. "Let me up."

"We are not letting you leave. Nurse! Nurse!" my dad yelled toward the hallway for backup.

A rather large and incredibly tall female nurse heard the commotion from down the hall and quickly entered the room.

"You listen here, young man, you're not going

anywhere," she informed me as she flipped me over in one swift move and shot me in the butt with a hefty dose of Ativan to calm me down.

With my nose pressed against the pillow, I tried to fight her off, but she had both my hands pinned behind my back. I could not move.

"This should do the trick," the nurse assured my parents.

Just before she stuck me with the needle, I looked over at my mom. She covered her mouth with both hands, and tears ran down her face. I turned my head to the other side when I felt the stick of the needle.

Almost immediately, I fell asleep.

I woke up three days later in my parents' bed.

৵৵৵

My dad had already worked it out with the insurance company. The treatment center my parents chose for me cost $27,000 for 28 days, and they would pay what our insurance did not cover. How they were going to swing it, I had no idea, but they were committed to getting me help. My parents took me to treatment.

If I go to treatment, I won't go to prison. The police are zeroing in on me, and I could face up to 10 years in prison for what I'm doing.

Even my drug supplier had pulled me aside and told me he'd seen guys like me slip into a darkness they could not climb out from underneath.

"You need to slow it down before you go too far," he warned me.

I'm only doing this to avoid prison. I'm not addicted. I'm fine.

Ready or not, I had 28 days to begin to figure out how I'd fallen so far, so fast.

ৡৡৡ

The treatment center was a 12-step program and encouraged participants to draw strength from a higher power. For some, that was God; for others, it could have been anything they considered to be bigger than themselves. It was the first time I had been introduced to spirituality as a source of strength. So I embraced "spirituality" and started learning about Transcendental Meditation, Buddhism, Shamanism and Christianity.

One of the things we were asked to confront and consider while in treatment was how the drugs we put on the streets affected other people.

"Did you ever stop to consider what the cocaine you were selling was doing to the lives of the people who were buying it on the streets? Maybe even trying it for the first time?" my counselor Marty probed.

"No, I didn't," I answered.

"How would you feel if your younger brothers and sisters were using the cocaine you had provided to your dealers? How many vehicle accidents or, even worse, deaths could have happened or did happen while people were under the influence of the drugs you sold? How many people are unrecognizable to the people who love them most because of the damage the cocaine you sold them has done? How many people overdosed and died from the cocaine you supplied them?"

I had never considered these things, and I was forced to admit how my actions had affected other people. I was forced to consider how much damage I had done to other people and to myself. Guilt started to mount, and I began to think about a life free of drugs.

As my time at the treatment center progressed, it felt good to be sober. It had been years since I'd gone more than a day or two without getting high or drinking alcohol. Sobriety became my new high.

Just as I took an extreme approach to pot and cocaine, I took the same approach to getting clean. When I got out, I wanted to start school to be a substance abuse counselor and eventually have my own practice. Even in my recovery, I took to extremes.

Not long after my treatment started, I was diagnosed with depression, ADHD and drug-induced paranoid schizophrenia. The doctor assigned to my case at the treatment center explained to me that people who use drugs with diagnoses like mine were called "chronic relapsers" and were much more likely to use again than people who did not have such diagnoses.

He prescribed several medications and told me that the meds would help combat the chemical imbalances that had been instrumental in leading me to drug abuse.

When my 28 days were up, I felt ready to go home and get on with my life.

"We highly recommend that you continue your recovery and move into one of the transitionary living houses on campus," Marty told me. "I don't think you are ready to go back home yet."

"No, I'm good. I'm ready," I insisted.

"Are you sure?" he said with concern.

"I'll find a sponsor and stay involved in AA. I can do this," I tried convincing him.

"That needs to be the first thing you do. Find some good meetings in your area, go every day, get a sponsor and work the steps."

I left against the recommendation of all involved in my treatment, but I felt certain I could withstand the temptations of the outside and quickly did as Marty recommended. I even started taking classes and working toward my counseling degree while living at home and working for my dad. I was on the right track, and six months into my sobriety, I convinced myself that I could handle a night out with some of my old friends.

ॐॐॐ

"Man, John. You look great!" one friend said.

"Yeah, dude. You had us worried, but you look like you've even put on a little weight. Good for you, man," another friend added.

"Yeah, I feel good. Six months sober. I've been at it for a while," I boasted.

I was sitting on the back porch at a party with all my pot-smoking friends who were already drunk, telling me how great it was that I was sober.

I strolled into the house and sat down at the kitchen table. It was a familiar scene with the music blaring, people laughing and drinking, and I could smell the pot smoke filling the air. My dance with drugs and alcohol was about to begin again.

"I'm going to get drunk tonight," I proclaimed to the already drunk girl sitting across from me at the table as I picked up the liquor bottle in front of me.

"Go ahead," she replied, shrugging her shoulders, completely unaware of the depths from which I had come and would soon return.

I got drunk, smoked a lot of pot and dry-heaved in the bathroom most of the night. At one point I asked for cocaine, but no one had any or I would have done that, too.

I woke up the next morning in the hallway outside of the bathroom next to some girl, knowing I would have to tell my parents and realizing I did not have a handle on my drug and alcohol use. I was powerless over my addiction.

When I walked in the door of my house, the guilt tumbled down on me. I was at a loss for words and knew I'd thrown all my hard work away. I felt disgusted. Adding to my guilt, I realized I had missed an obligation to my brothers and sister.

My parents had counted on me to be home with the

kids that night while they were out of town, but I blew them off to party.

You don't have to tell anyone.

No one has to know you relapsed.

I tried telling myself I could keep it a secret, but I knew I needed help and could not get through it alone. I did not want to go back to the life I'd been living while using drugs, and I knew there was no in-between place for me. I knew I would go all the way back and in a hurry. The only choice I had, if I wanted to survive it, was to come clean with my parents, call my sponsor, go to a meeting and start all over again.

And that's what I did.

゠゠゠

My addiction had a hold on me, and I feared I could not break free.

Within two months, I was feeling so depressed and hopeless that my doctor decided to change my medication in an effort to help get my mental disorders sorted out.

"This one has a tendency to make people feel speedy, so let me know right away if you have this type of reaction and need to change the medication," my doctor warned.

Speedy? That won't work for me. I should tell him not to prescribe it.

But I did not admit to the red flag that was clearly waving in front of me.

"Okay, I will let you know," I answered without

showing any reservations about using the newly prescribed drug.

The next day I took my first pill as prescribed, and I immediately felt what the doctor had described, but I did not call him when I experienced the "speedy" feeling. Instead, I called Scott, and he picked me up at my house for the first time since I had left treatment.

On my way to Scott's car, I popped another "speedy" pill and went to find some cocaine.

કે કે કે

It would be easy for me to blame my second relapse on the medication prescribed to me, but I knew as soon as the doctor warned of its side effects that I should not have risked taking it. Someone committed to long-term recovery would have spoken up and said something, but I was starting the dance again.

Within minutes, Scott and I had bought an 8-ball of cocaine, which is 3.5 grams. Minutes after, I was high with the old, familiar feeling of wanting more and more.

Instantly, the paranoia set in again. Only this time, it was even worse, probably because of all the medications I was taking. I thought I was going to die because I had used up all the "chances" God gave me, and my death would serve as an example of what happens when people don't take their second chances in life seriously. As much as I knew this night was probably going to kill me, I could not stop. When we ran out of cocaine, I wanted more.

"Come on, dude," I tried convincing Scott. "Let's go get some more."

"No, dude. Let's just chill and smoke some pot."

I wanted no part of it and kept bugging Scott and the other guys to take me to an ATM to get some money and buy us more blow. When they would not agree to take me, I started thinking of ways to get more. I thought about stealing it from a dealer I knew, already willing to break my own code of ethics when it came to doing drugs.

When the girls we were with told me they were going to the store to get some food, I agreed to go.

I'll just get some money from the ATM and find a ride to get more coke.

I got in the car thinking I would fool them, but as soon as we pulled into the parking lot of the store, I knew they had fooled me when I saw my dad's truck.

"You called my dad?" I asked. "Why'd you do that?"

"Dude, you're scaring us. You need to get some help," Scott told me, admitting they had arranged to have my dad pick me up when I would not stop hounding them to buy more cocaine.

As I approached his truck, I thought about running and felt to make sure I had my wallet and phone.

"Here we are again, John," my dad said to me. No matter the struggles he and my mom had suffered through with their own addictions, as my father, he wanted better for me.

His face showed his obvious disappointment, and in that moment, I felt too tired to run.

All of a sudden, I could not bear another day of using cocaine.

જાજાજા

When I got home, my mom was crying. I hugged her and went to bed. I woke up on and off feeling restless and afraid. Then I noticed a shelf next to the bed full of my mom's recovery books.

I felt weak and tired, so tired of the running I had been doing while chasing the high. I desperately tried to escape the pain that could no longer be remedied with a puff of this or a line of that.

My tired legs carried me to the bathroom where I dropped in desperation to my knees. I could not take another day. I knew I would surely die if I did not get help, but I was beaten down by my failure to remain sober after finishing treatment, and seeing my mom's recovery books on the shelf only reminded me of my failure. I feared I would always be an addict trying to manage his addiction and failing miserably. I had no more answers. I was lost. I was defeated. I was ready to change, but I did not know how to save myself, so in my final attempt to find my way out of the abyss of addiction, I said the only words I had left to say.

"Jesus, if you are real, save me."

I sobbed those words.

When I finally stood up, I felt a change. I suddenly felt happy, like I had hope. I couldn't remember the last time I'd felt hopeful.

Every destructive thing I'd ever done to myself felt like it was falling away. As a kid, I'd always felt lonely, but in that moment, I felt like God was with me. I knew all about God — I'd talked to him when I was young — but it all started to seem different. I embraced the idea of allowing God to be a part of my life and help me through my addictions. I embraced the idea of a loving God who listened to me even when I felt like I was falling apart. I knew I couldn't manage to give up the drugs and alcohol on my own. It was time to give up control of my life and hand it over to God.

I left my parents' bathroom and did not tell anyone right away. When I did tell my dad what I had done, he embraced me. A few days later, he gave me a Bible with my name on it.

Nana, my grandmother, had been praying for me for a long time. She even came to visit me when I was in treatment.

"John, now you stay close to God, honey," she told me when I told her on the phone about my prayer on the bathroom floor. "He will never leave you."

"I know, Nana. Thank you."

Nana started sending me Bible verses in the mail, and we often talked on the phone about how I was doing. I started going to church, and that led me to a young adult's group called All Things New, which I attended every Saturday night. I was still going to AA meetings at that time, but little by little, church events started replacing meetings. I felt whole and renewed and, unlike when I left treatment, I had no desire for drugs or alcohol since the day on the bathroom floor when I prayed that simple prayer — *Jesus, if you are real, save me.*

~~~

Even though I was sober, I still had a lot of wreckage in my life to clean up and bad habits to unlearn. Thankfully, about a year after I got sober, my friend's parents from church, Mike and Theresa, started mentoring me. They taught me valuable life skills, like how to do a budget and how to pay off debt. They also taught me the importance of being to work on time, being a reliable employee and how to make better life decisions — things I'd never learned while dealing drugs. They became like second parents to me.

Their teachings prepared me for a job in sales when the opportunity came up. "I think you've got a lot of potential," Christine told me. "We're going to take a chance on you."

Christine knew someone from my church and had been in business for more than 20 years. I had no experience in sales, but Christine liked me so the company paid for all of my training and taught me that sales did not have to be pushy or degrading when done with integrity. I was a fast learner and moved my way up the corporate ladder, earning decent money and making something of myself at the office job I'd been dreaming about.

Meanwhile, I continued to attend the church's

services, small group discussions and social activities. I was not dating anyone. Shortly after committing my life to God, I started talking with an old friend Laura. She was a Christian and we clicked, so I thought we were meant to be together. I ended up moving to Wyoming for her and sleeping with her, but then we broke up. I felt horrible because I knew I shouldn't be having sex outside of marriage.

The experience with Laura helped me realize that sexual restraint was still a problem in my life, even though the drugs weren't anymore.

After we broke up, I went to a Christian youth conference called Generation Unleashed. The pastor was preaching on purity, and I responded to God's tug on my heart when he gave the altar call. I was delivered from sexual temptations — pornography and fornication — that night and never returned to it. This allowed me to become even closer to God because I could approach him in prayer without feeling guilty about secret sins. I made the decision I would not get involved with another woman until I was ready for marriage. I focused on rebuilding my life with God at its center. I knew that when the time came for me to settle down and start a family, I would be a better man for the choice I had made.

かかか

Joy and I had been friends for several years. I met her at the young adults group when I first started going to church. After a long time developing a healthy friendship, Joy and I started talking about dating each other.

I was reluctant because I still was not looking for a relationship, but my feelings for Joy had grown over time.

As I considered the years Joy and I spent in true friendship, it became impossible to deny my feelings for her, so I went to Joy's father for permission to date his daughter, and with his blessing, I had flowers delivered to her at work.

Joy and I dated for just a few months before I proposed to her.

I wanted the proposal to be special, so I took her on a dinner cruise.

"It's a beautiful night," I told her, my palms sweaty and shaking with nervousness as the two of us stood on the deck, looking across the water to the city skyline.

"Yes, it is," Joy agreed.

That moment, I decided to get on one knee and ask her to be my wife.

"Where did you go?" She laughed as I disappeared from her line of sight when she turned back from looking at the water.

"I'm here," I said as I held her right hand in mine and asked her to marry me.

I was so nervous, I had not even noticed that I had taken her by the wrong hand and placed the ring on the wrong finger.

"Yes!" she spoke softly with delight.

In just five years, God took me from being a lonely,

depressed cocaine addict to being the husband of my best friend. And all because I laid my life before him on a bathroom floor and prayed this simple prayer with all of my heart: *Jesus, if you are real, save me.*

❧❧❧

It came time to either work my way up to management or to make a career change before we had children and greater responsibilities, which might have made me cautious about risking a bold career move. As much as I enjoyed my co-workers and appreciated Christine taking a chance by hiring me, I knew that I would not be happy in that field of work for the rest of my life. I started dreaming of building a business of my own, so that's what I set out to do. We paid off all our debt to minimize the risks of quitting my secure job, but it was still a tough first year in business with a lot of ups and downs. In time, it became obvious that I could make it profitable and that I'd made the right decision.

It wasn't my first time as an entrepreneur — only this time, I was making an honest living. Long gone were the days of selling drugs to make a buck so I could score a hit.

❧❧❧

Just a year after leaving my job and starting my own business, Joy gave birth to our daughter.

The moment she was born, I felt overwhelmed by

God's grace. He had forgiven me for my past and set me on a new path, bringing me to this moment with our daughter.

My daughter and my wife will never see me high. They will never have to see me as I was when I was lost and barely treading a sea of darkness. You did that, God. Your grace saved me.

When our second daughter was born just a couple years later, I was even more overwhelmed by my blessings.

Our church, Church on the Rock, leads a service at the local prison, Larch Correctional Facility, as part of its ministry. I began helping with Sunday services each month at the men's prison. Usually, about 30 to 40 men showed up, and sometimes as many as 50. I sometimes told the men my story.

"There were times I didn't want people. I just wanted to be alone with cocaine," I told them. "I wanted to sell more so I could do more, and I had no interest in anyone or anything getting in the way of me and cocaine. Not food. Not sex. Not family. Not God. Not anything."

The men looked at me like they understood everything I said and have been where I have been. I never told them to impress them with how far I have come — I just wanted them to know what God could do.

"There's a difference between being completely delivered from addiction and managing addiction."

"Amen," some of the men would say.

"Managing can work. And it's better than the life I was living. It's tough having to face the temptations and live with my addictive tendencies day after day," I explained. "But when I realized that God had freed me from the desire to ever use drugs and alcohol again, I was signed up for life."

At the end of some of the talks I gave about my own story, people sometimes came up and said that hearing my story gave them hope for their own lives.

"That's good," I said. "Because hope is the first thing that God gave to me, and that's a good place to start."

PING-PONG AND BALLET SHOES
THE STORY OF DREW AND ABIGAIL
WRITTEN BY KAREN KOCZWARA

No. This can't be happening.

I re-read the email, my heart thudding and sinking with every word.

Drew. My beloved husband. Carrying this terrible secret our entire marriage.

How could he do this to me?

We're meant to be together forever.

What will happen to us now?

I caught my reflection in the mirror, and my shock turned to disgust and self-hatred.

If I wasn't so fat and ugly, maybe this never would have happened.

I must be doing something wrong.

This must all be my fault.

࿐࿐࿐

Abigail

I was born in Provo, Utah. The middle of nine siblings, I grew up with seven sisters and a brother. My father worked in the technology and finance industry, while my mother stayed home with us. A strict Mormon family, we enjoyed living in an area primarily dominated by those who followed our Mormon faith. Provo, home to Brigham Young University, also boasted acres of hills and mountains, perfect for summertime hiking and fishing and wintertime snow skiing. It was, in essence, a picture-perfect paradise for a little girl. But a storm brewed beyond the rolling green hills and blue skies, one that would subtly sweep me into its wake and hold me captive for years.

As a young boy, my father was exposed to pornography at the age when most boys have just learned to ride a bike. His parents never addressed the issue, and it warped his view of sexuality well into his adult years. He married my mother and began a family of his own. But over the years, he physically, emotionally and sexually abused me and my siblings.

Sometimes, my father flew into a rage, throwing me across the room and slamming me against the wall when he grew angry. One day, my sisters and I giggled happily while washing dishes together. Annoyed by our chatter, my father slapped me across the face. The sting in my heart lasted long after the sting on my cheek disappeared.

My mother served as the disciplinarian, grounding us and sending us to our rooms whenever we misbehaved. As a faithful Mormon wife, she performed all her duties diligently, canning foods, cooking fine meals and teaching us how to play musical instruments. The house remained tidy to perfection, and we could not walk out the door unless everything was in its place. Though she did her best to manage a full brood of kids, she lacked emotional intimacy and often hurt my feelings. Especially critical and distrusting, she quickly pointed out my faults.

"I'm no artist, but I think you could fix this or this," my mother said when I brought home my artwork from school.

My heart sank as I watched her brow furrow in disapproval. Though I loved to draw, I began pointing out the flaws of my work before she could, not wanting to endure her criticism. Nothing, it seemed, was good enough.

There were plenty of happy moments between the bad. My parents both had their good points. I loved the sense of camaraderie that came with being part of a large family, the bonds that could not be broken. In the evenings, we sat around the piano, harmonizing to the tunes and laughing. There were trips to Disneyland, Idaho and even Barbados. My father taught me how to snow ski, and I loved the feeling of flying down the mountain with powder in my face. In the summer, we slept in a tree in the front yard making a big nest with our mattresses between the branches. As I grew older, my sisters and I did odd jobs to earn money for the summer matinee movies. Life, in many ways, seemed idyllic, reminiscent of Andy Griffith's Mayberry. To those looking in, we were one big, happy family.

Our Mormon faith sat at the very center of our family, directing every aspect of our daily life. I loved growing up in the Mormon Church, believing from a young age we belonged to the one and only true church. I knew and believed the basics — Mormonism was founded in the early 1800s by a man named Joseph Smith, seen by his followers as a modern-day prophet. After his death, followers of the faith accepted Brigham Young as their new leader and emigrated to what became Utah Territory. Mormons focused heavily on family, believing that one purpose of earthly life was to learn to choose good over evil. They sought to live good lives, modeled after God.

Community service was a large part of my religion and a large part of my family life as well. We attended weekly church services and participated in several ordinances, or religious rituals. Naming and blessing children, anointing and blessing the sick and participating in special temple ceremonies were just a few of our regular practices.

At age 8, I was baptized into the Mormon Church, vowing to follow the ways of my religion for the rest of my life. I was happy to commit — as far as I was concerned, Mormonism was the best and only way to live. Someday, I'd have a family of my own, leading my children down the same path. There was, I thought, no other way.

Despite belonging to a big family and church, I often felt alone, ugly and unappreciated. I believed my sisters were prettier and smarter, and it seemed I could do nothing right. My mother's criticism and my father's emotional disconnect weighed me down, and I struggled to find peace within myself. As I grew older, my father referred to me and my sisters as "hot" and referenced us becoming models. His words made me uncomfortable. I did not want to be "hot" — I just wanted to be loved. And it was hard to feel loved when my father's harsh hands reminded me I was not good enough.

By seventh grade, I decided to find a way to get noticed. Kids at school noticed I was skinny, and I enjoyed the attention. *Maybe I could get even skinner,* I decided. I began skipping meals, surviving on water, apples and a few crackers. I didn't count calories. I simply avoided food. Food equaled fat, and I did not want to get fat.

Soon, my clothes began to fall off me. Instead of hiding behind baggy sweatshirts and pants, I proudly displayed my new figure, hoping my peers would notice my shrinking frame. When they did, I felt secretly pleased. I'd lost weight but gained an audience at last.

When I was 15, we took a family trip to Disneyland. I sat in the backseat with my brother during the long drive. As I drifted off to sleep, I suddenly felt his hands slide near me, touching me in places I knew weren't right. I cringed, frightened. *What is he doing? This isn't okay.* I never breathed a word of the incident to anyone and wrote off my brother as just a horny kid who couldn't keep his hands to himself.

For my 16th birthday, my parents presented me with the opportunity of a lifetime — dance lessons at a local studio. My heart surged with excitement at the idea of pursuing my dream. I attended my first lesson in a basement facility, then went out and bought new clothes and shoes to dance in. With so many children to feed, my parents rarely paid for extracurricular activities. I would not take the lessons for granted.

RESCUE

On my third lesson, I happily headed to the studio, only to discover that the place had shut down. The instructor had run off with my mother's check, and my short-lived dream had been shattered.

As I neared high school graduation, I continued watching what I ate, consuming as little food as possible. My friend confronted me about my behavior one day.

"I'm going to tell your mother you have an eating disorder," she said.

To my horror, she did. A few nights later, my parents called all of my siblings into my bedroom for a family meeting.

"Abby has something to share with us," my mom announced, her eyes meeting mine.

I gulped, not wanting to talk. *Why is she doing this, humiliating me in front of everyone?*

When I did not speak, my mother piped up. "From now on, we will not be inviting Abby to the dinner table. She won't be eating with us anymore."

I sat there, stunned. *I can't believe my little sisters are hearing this when they have no clue what she means.*

My mother turned back to me. "I know you are just doing this for attention, Abigail, and we will not give it to you."

The family left my room, and I collapsed onto the bed, sobbing. A while later, my father came down and tried to comfort me.

"I'm sorry about that, Abby," he said gently.

For a moment, I felt understood. I smiled, grateful for

my father's sympathetic gesture. My mother and I avoided each other for the next few weeks, not sure how to respond to the spectacle she'd made of me. Food remained the enemy, but in all other aspects of my life, I remained a good girl. I attended youth group faithfully, did not drink, do drugs or have sex with boys. Occasionally, a lie or a few disrespectful words slipped out of my mouth, but I completed the Sunday sacrament ritual to repent and be aligned with God. I read scripture faithfully and prayed. The Mormon faith described Jesus as my brother and God as my heavenly father. I did not want to upset either of them. As far as the church was concerned, I was on the right track, performing my dutiful service, remaining pure for my husband someday. But an ache had formed in my heart, one that could not be filled by rituals and prayers and doing good deeds. I did not understand the longing. I only knew the pain that kept spreading like a cancer, seeping into my veins, reminding me I was not okay.

I graduated high school and started classes at a community college two hours away. College offered all the freedom and fun I'd longed for. Without my parents lurking over my shoulder, I could do as I pleased. Happy for any attention guys threw my way, I began making out with them, always careful to never go too far.

I developed a compulsive exercise regimen, running miles a day, and I also started to drink alcohol. My eating problems worsened. I began lying to gain people's pity. When the guilt ate away at me, I went to the bishop to confess my wrongdoings. After one year, I returned home.

"Let's find you a job," my mother suggested. "With the money you earn, you should buy a guitar."

I loved music and had hoped to buy my own guitar with my summer earnings.

One day, I headed to the music store with my mother to browse. While wandering through the guitar section, I spotted a cute guy a few feet away. On instinct, I glanced down at his hand and noticed his bare ring finger. *He's single,* I thought, my heart soaring.

"Do you play or sing?" I asked him, making polite conversation.

"I play," he replied with a smile.

He took me in the sound room and began playing a few tunes on the guitar. *Wow, this guy is cute, and he plays a mean guitar. What more could you ask for?*

"I'm Abigail," I said.

"Drew."

My mother found me, and I introduced her to Drew. When we got back into the car, she asked me if I'd given him my phone number.

"No," I replied with a shrug. "If he wants to date me, he'll find me."

While I was out on a date with another guy that night, Drew called my house. My parents delivered the message when I got home.

"You should hang out with him," they said. "He seems like a good guy."

I agreed to go out with Drew, and to my delight, I discovered we had much in common. After three months of dating, he proposed. In typical Mormon fashion, we planned a short engagement. We married in the Mormon Temple in Salt Lake City. The ceremony included a variety of rituals as we committed to a lifetime of purity and faithfulness. We wore the Mormon ceremonial clothing, kneeling at the altar as the officiant, a temple sealer, spoke over us. We were then pronounced husband and wife for all eternity.

The ceremony seemed beautiful. As a faithful Mormon girl, I grew up believing marriage was the ultimate earthly goal. Drew and I would bear children together, and those children would make up our eternal family in heaven someday. I recited, "He is mine, and I am his," promising to give myself fully to my husband for all of time. I believed we'd begun our journey of bliss, embarking on a road to everlasting happiness and faithfulness to God. But the ring on my finger and the man at my side did not ease the ache in my heart. And it would be years before I'd learn how to truly fill that empty hole.

☙☙☙

Drew

Like Abigail's upbringing, mine was, in many ways, the quintessential all-American happy home. I grew up in a house in the woods outside Salem, Oregon, one of six children in a large Mormon family. Movie nights, sled rides, trampoline fun, sporting events, youth group and scouting activities filled my childhood. My father was a dentist, while my mother worked as a dental hygienist. We never lacked for anything. When it came time for each child to drive, a car was always available. Hearty homemade meals made their way to the dinner table most nights, along with plenty of laughter, too.

My parents both grew up in homes where they were taught Christian values. They attended Bible camps some summers, but their parents didn't discuss God much around the house. My father's mother passed away of cancer when he was 14, and his father married four more times. The family structure crumbled, as he and his brothers were left to their own devices. Eventually, his father killed himself, a tragedy I learned of from a family friend years later. My father rarely spoke of the painful incident.

After meeting in college, my parents got involved in Campus Crusade for Christ, a popular Christian program on campus. When they married, they wrote their own vows, suggesting they be married even after death. When a friend gave them a copy of the Book of Mormon and discussed the church's teaching, the message resonated with them, particularly the part about being "sealed for eternity." They embraced Mormonism, converting and becoming "sealed in the temple" a year later. As first-generation Mormons, they vowed to raise their children in the faith and to pass their beliefs on to generations to come.

At 8, the age of accountability, I was baptized into the Mormon Church. At age 12, I was ordained into the priesthood, an honorable rite. The elders in the church laid hands on me, preparing me for my higher calling in the church. My responsibilities were to my fellow youth. I became active in Boy Scouts, working my way toward Eagle Scout merit. Like Abigail, I sought to be a good Mormon teen, proceeding with all the rituals, attending weekly services and saying my prayers. I knew no other way.

The year I turned 15, I began messing around with girls, making out with them and crossing the forbidden lines. I knew my actions were wrong — I was to remain pure until marriage. That summer, my buddies introduced me to pornography, and it planted an appetite for the vice inside me.

The occasional dirty movie or magazine sparked my curiosity as well. After touching myself in ways I'd been taught were inappropriate, I quickly felt guilty for what I'd done. I went to counseling for repentance, hoping I'd stop, but the counseling only helped temporarily. Looking at pornography and making out with girls became a regular part of my life. *I'm not as bad as that guy,* I often reasoned, thinking of my friends who'd crossed much more serious lines. But the guilt still gnawed at me, and I wondered how a good Mormon boy like me had found himself being tempted to violate my moral code.

I graduated high school, and after a year of college, I prepared to serve on a mission to New Zealand. Upon turning 19, boys in the Mormon Church were strongly encouraged to leave their families and embark on a two-year mission to various places around the globe. The purpose was to proselytize, or share the Mormon faith with others they met, as well as perform acts of service and good will. We did not get to choose our mission destination — it was chosen for us. I'd watched other boys in the church go through this process and knew my time would eventually come. Fulfilling my mission would bring me one step closer to becoming a more faithful priesthood holder in the Mormon Church.

As I prepared to go, however, my guilt over the pornography continued to weigh on me. Embarking on a mission required complete cleansing, and I was far from clean. I disclosed my sin to the bishop, and he counseled me, saying I must qualify for God's mercy, grace and forgiveness.

"The Father in heaven delivers the law of justice," the church taught. "Jesus exists to satisfy the Father's demands. Through repentance and faithful work, you can receive the mercy and grace Jesus offers and be forgiven. You will sin again tomorrow and no longer be justified or worthy, so repent again and be forgiven."

I knew the drill. Though the teaching sounded solid, pleasing God seemed to be a never-ending game of ping-pong between my Savior and heavenly father. I messed up, then Jesus had to go and work things out with God, and then I waited, hoping my repentance was sincere enough for God to accept me again. The process exhausted me.

At the end of the day, after all the repenting and the cleansing and the promising to not mess up again, I felt better, but as soon as I messed up again, I felt rotten again. The shame and guilt became a subtle burden I carried for years.

Shortly before I left for New Zealand, I went to a missionary training center for three weeks, where I learned how to tell other people about my Mormon faith. A week and a half into the training, exhaustion and guilt overwhelmed me so strongly I thought I might collapse. *I am not worthy of being a missionary representing Jesus Christ,* I thought to myself, tears streaming down my cheeks. *I have not confessed all my sins. How can I go into another part of the world and share my faith when I've been such a mess?*

I turned the corner and headed into the dorm bathroom. At that moment, something strange and miraculous happened. I glanced in the mirror and saw a broken 19-year-old kid, and I doubled over to the ground crying. And then, I felt a comforting warmth, which I believed came only from the loving arms of Jesus. *I am here, and I forgive you,* I felt him say to me. The moment was deep, intense and absolutely real. I was not dreaming or conjuring up some fantasy. I believe I felt the arms of Jesus wrap around me, and I experienced his merciful love for the very first time in my life.

The incident stayed with me long after it ended. I had experienced Jesus, no doubt in my mind. This was not the sort of trivial experience I'd had in the church, going through the motions of confession. This was something much more powerful, something tangible, something lasting. This was the real Jesus, I thought, speaking to me as a loving father gently speaks to his son. I would not forget it as long as I lived.

I went on my mission, trying to stay pure and clean throughout my time away. But I struggled with touching myself inappropriately. The cycle of guilt and disgust continued. *Why could I not break free from this habit?*

The summer I left for my mission, my father sent me a letter, revealing some shocking news. He had been viewing pornography and engaged in an extramarital affair. Like me, he bore his own guilty secrets. Rattled, I drove to my mission president's house, where he counseled and prayed a special blessing over me. I returned to business, trying to focus on my mission. My father and I corresponded, and he told me he and my mother planned to stay together. But the affair remained a stain on our home, one we could not easily remove and forget about.

I returned from my mission, determined to focus on my Mormon faith and not think about girls.

But before long, I began dating, involving myself in a bad relationship. After breaking up with the girl, I told God, "I want to meet my bride."

I knew of two girls I wanted to date, so I made a contract with God. I committed to prayer and acts of worthiness, deciding not to date anyone until summer while asking God to prepare me to meet my future wife.

Neither of those girls proved to be the one for me. Instead, the first week of summer break, I met a pretty girl at a music store, and we struck up a conversation over guitars. Just a few months later, I pledged eternity to her in the Mormon temple. It was the best decision I'd ever made in my life.

But "happily ever after" did not come the way we expected. Instead, we began an exciting, harrowing and surprising journey neither of us could have conjured in our wildest dreams.

ल ल ल

Abigail

Just after Drew and I married, we moved to Oregon, where we could be closer to his family and he could pursue opportunities in business. Wanting to start our family right away, I became pregnant shortly after we wed. Still struggling with my long-term eating disorder, I grew anxious as my body began to change.

Panic ensued as my waist expanded and my clothes became too tight. I fervently watched what I ate, afraid to gain too much weight.

Anxiety and depression overwhelmed me, followed by extreme negative self-talk. I did not like myself at all. Drew was a wonderful husband, but even he could not alleviate the low self-esteem I'd struggled with all my life.

Though Drew's family was thrilled to have us close by, I grew sad and lonely in our new state. Drew spent long hours working, while I spent long hours missing my family back home. In October, I gave birth to our first child, a beautiful baby girl. Two years later, we welcomed another little girl into our home. Drew threw himself into a new business venture, and I focused on our children and the home. Though lonely, I tried not to complain or pick fights with Drew or otherwise cause turmoil in our house. I hated the yelling I'd endured in my childhood home, and I did not want to repeat that for my children.

Shortly after my second daughter's birth, I learned of my parents' divorce. The news shocked me. I didn't know of my mother's struggle with depression, of the years she'd tried to keep a brave face while her marriage slowly unraveled. *Weren't we supposed to be the good Mormon family? Weren't they supposed to be sealed for eternity? What would happen to my family now?*

As Drew's business expanded, we moved to Washington. As is typical in the Mormon faith, we found the ward, or church congregation, close to our house and began attending. I became pregnant again, this time enjoying every second. I decided to embrace the weight I gained instead of fearing it. This time, I gave birth to a little boy. It seemed perhaps we were headed toward our happily ever after — three great kids, a thriving business and a solid marriage.

And then I learned Drew's secret.

June rolled around, bringing with it the first hints of summer. The dreary Washington skies cleared, the gray rolling away as the sun peeked over the mountains. Drew sent me an email one day on his way home from work, explaining that he'd struggled with resisting the urge to view pornography for years.

"I'm going to meet with our bishop when I get home," he added.

My heart dropped, and my entire body froze. *This can't be right! When we married, we were sealed for eternity together. He is my celestial companion. This is beyond devastating!*

Drew returned home and left right away for his appointment with the bishop. I remained frozen, unsure how to respond. Surprisingly, I did not feel angry or bitter. Instead, I felt ashamed of myself. *Surely, I must have done something wrong. Maybe it's because I'm so fat and ugly that he's turned to pornography. That must be it.*

The next day, I grilled Drew. "Okay, tell me everything. I need to know."

Slowly, ashamedly, Drew told me how he'd been exposed to pornography as a boy and had been tempted to view it since he was a teen. I watched his face fall as he recounted the details — how he'd battled with guilt and strived to repent, repeatedly going to the bishop for confession, being strong for a while, only to do it again and again. He chose his words carefully, telling me when and how much, even disclosing what types of online pornography he'd viewed.

"I love you, Abby. And I understand if you are hurt and angry."

"I am so sad for you, Drew," I said quietly. "I'm sad you couldn't share this with me before."

Drew hung his head. Neither of us knew what to say, how to act. Suddenly, we were two strangers in a room, this secret in the open for the very first time. What was I to do with this shocking information?

The days passed, and instead of growing upset with Drew, I grew more upset with myself. I avoided my reflection in the mirror, disgusted with my looks. Shame seeped in next. I slept as far away from him as possible, scooting to the edge of the bed at night. When he tried to reach for my hand, I quickly pulled it away. Drew remained respectful of my space, not wanting to push himself on me. We drifted through the house, the silence deafening, both of us wounded and unsure how to take the next step.

I didn't know how I'd ever trust Drew again. I pulled away from sexual intimacy, not interested in giving myself over to a man I wasn't sure I knew. *How can I ever be vulnerable with this guy again? I gave him my heart, my soul, my body for all eternity! What now?*

I threw myself into my house and my children, being the best mother and homemaker I could be. Meanwhile, the economy tanked and, with it, Drew's business. Two months after he disclosed his secret, we lost the business and were forced to move out of our house. We moved in with his parents in Salem, Oregon. Gradually, we became intimate again, and I became pregnant with our fourth child. When fall rolled around, I began homeschooling our older children, and in May the following year, I gave birth to another little boy. In just a short time, we'd endured a whirlwind of both joyous and devastating events, and I was about to crash hard.

PING-PONG AND BALLET SHOES

The depression took root. Living with Drew's parents, trying to school two children and care for two young ones, all the while struggling financially, proved challenging. At last, we found a place of our own to rent, and the money slowly trickled in again. Despite our trials, we looked forward to the future and wanted to work hard at building our family the best we could.

The following November, I met some new friends through a homeschooling program. Many of them were Christians who talked openly about their relationship with Jesus Christ. I watched them intently, intrigued by the way they talked and prayed. They spoke of Jesus not just as a figure of their religion, but as a real being, one who cared about the details of their lives. This idea wasn't new to me, but I had never experienced it like that before. The Mormon Church often talked about Jesus Christ. The words weren't much different, but these people's hearts were. They seemed more sincere, more hopeful, more intimate in their prayers. *Was I missing something?*

I listened as my new friends prayed, mesmerized by their posture and words. While my prayers were sincere, theirs were sincere on another level — beautiful, personal and almost romantic. *They pray like they really know Jesus, like he's their best friend or something. I wish I had that.*

I sank further into my depression, confused about my new feelings regarding my faith. I had always been so sure of my Mormon religion, had never questioned it before. But suddenly, my tidy box was coming undone, and I wasn't sure what to do with it. *What if I'm not on the right path? What if my eternal fate is not what I always assumed it would be?* I sank to a low, growing even more confused and unhappy. I tried to shake it off, convincing myself it was just me feeling overwhelmed about our finances, the kids, homeschooling and Drew's pornography addiction. But the questions lingered, hanging in the air, beckoning for answers.

"I want to take a break from Mormonism," I confided to one of my new Christian friends one day. I could hardly believe the words had come out of my mouth. Everywhere we'd moved, I'd always gotten involved in our ward, pursuing my "calling," or assigned tasks. Kids' ministry and music had always been a favorite of mine. But now I desired something more — something deeper. How could I grow close to my heavenly father and Jesus Christ?

"Abby, take a break," my Christian friend encouraged me. "One of our pastors took a break for a whole year and just focused on God and prayed."

I mulled over her words. For the first time, I finally understood what I was lacking — a true relationship with God. I wanted intimacy with Jesus Christ, not just a bunch of rules and regulations. Sure, I'd done lots of decent things in my life, and sure, I'd always been a pretty good Mormon girl, but where had that really gotten me? I'd struggled my whole life with lack of self-worth, never feeling good enough for God or anyone else. I often felt empty and alone, despite trying to do everything right. I had a beautiful family, but even that wasn't enough to fill the gaping hole in my heart. Something was surely missing, and I wanted to find out what that was.

That December, we received a 30-day notice at our house when the landlord decided to sell it. With just weeks until Christmas, we'd been forced to move out. Where would we go?

"I know this guy up in Battle Ground who is losing his house to foreclosure," Drew told me. "Maybe we could work out a deal with him and his bank."

I agreed to the idea. Within days, the situation worked out perfectly.

We moved to Battle Ground a week before Christmas, trying to carry on with our normal celebrations for the children. The move aligned perfectly with my growing concerns about my Mormon faith. It was time to go off the grid for a while, to lay low and figure things out. I had no desire to leave "the true church," but I needed to know who God really was and what it meant to have a real relationship with him. I was ready to see where the new road led, even if it meant shaking up the safe bubble I'd lived in all my life.

かかか

Drew

The unraveling began for me when the business I'd worked so hard to build slowly came apart. I'd put everything into the business, even at the expense of my family. After revealing my pornography addiction to

Abigail, my marriage became deeply shaken. In the Mormon faith, we'd been taught we would be bonded together through eternity, even becoming gods in our next life. Could this possibly happen if Abigail and I were not on the same page in this earthly life?

One day, I sat in a restaurant with my buddy, having lunch. My friend turned to me and asked bluntly, "Do you take everything in the Mormon faith at face value?"

His question sparked something in me. On the outside, we were an upstanding Mormon family. I fulfilled my calling in the church as a lay minister, and Abigail fulfilled her calling as a wife, mother and helper with ministry as well. But in truth, we were a complete mess behind closed doors. Abigail struggled with low self-esteem and identity issues, and I could not break free from my sexual addiction. No matter what I did or how hard I tried, I felt like I was still watching the ping-pong game with God and Jesus, trying to earn grace. And I had begun to wonder, was grace really free? Or would I have to spend the rest of my life trying, failing, confessing and then trying some more? The whole game was getting a bit exhausting.

I joined a sexual addiction men's group. As I confessed my addiction to my peers, I learned of their struggles, too. But I also learned something especially important. This pornography issue had really been a medication, a way to avoid dealing with a failed identity. For the first time, I realized I didn't really know who I was as a man. For years, I had used pornography as a way to self-medicate. It felt good at the time, but in the end, I always wound up feeling guilty, depressed and more miserable. I was tired of the vicious cycle, and it seemed everyone else in the room was, too.

"Drew, what's your deepest identity?" one of the guys asked.

The question shocked me, and immediately I felt like God was speaking to my heart. *You are a mature Mormon. You serve, you strive and you know the doctrine. But can you really identify with me?*

I wanted to say, "I'm a Mormon. That's my identity." But was that really it? Was that the entire summary of my whole being? Suddenly, I wasn't so sure.

I drove home, confused and shaken. I could not get this experience out of my mind.

I read a book, *Wild at Heart,* by John Eldredge, which discussed men's identity in Christ. The book described the various stages in a man's life, starting when he is a young boy. It asserted that every man longs to answer one burning question, "Do I have what it takes?" Or more importantly, "Who am I, really?" I was starting to learn that those questions could only be answered by knowing God properly and intimately.

I recalled talking with several friends who professed a Christian faith. "You don't know the same Jesus I know," they told me.

I stared at them, perplexed. *You are the ones who are lost,* I concluded, feeling sorry for them. *You don't have the true church.*

I wrestled with it all. "Grace is a gift from Jesus. In fact, grace means free gift, unearned. If I put conditions on what I have to do to receive grace, it is no longer a free gift, it is an earned gift." I couldn't stop thinking about this. *If I earn it, it isn't really grace. If it isn't grace, then who is this Jesus I'm following? Wait, do I know the same Jesus?*

It rocked my faith. My beliefs, my identity and my Savior all came into question.

I thought back to the dorm bathroom when I first experienced Jesus forgiving me. That wasn't earned. Jesus found me when I first realized I was so messed up that I wasn't worthy of God. I called out to him, and he found me. The Bible told me that my very ability to cry out for God was grace moving in me. I wasn't satisfying some condition to be forgiven and saved.

I'd never questioned my Mormon faith, had always accepted it the way one does their hair color, their height or a birthmark. It was just a part of me and always had been since the beginning. I'd done everything a good Mormon boy does — been baptized, been ordained to the priesthood, gone on a mission and started my eternal family. I'd even defended my faith to my friends when they'd questioned it, convinced I belonged to the one true church. But I started having more questions than answers. My safe world began to crack, and there was no turning back.

PING-PONG AND BALLET SHOES

༒༒༒

Abigail

Drew and I continued questioning our faith and seeking the truth. We spoke to his brother to better understand his perspective. His brother had walked away from the Mormon Church years before to party, but he'd later discovered a relationship with Jesus.

"Things will never be the same if you leave," he told us candidly.

Fear gripped us both as we continued our journey. Our bishop wanted me to accept a new calling in youth ministry in the new ward, and I hesitated.

Drew confronted the bishop. "I'm not certain we should operate this way, always trying so hard to earn grace."

The bishop replied, "I hope you aren't deceived."

Deceived. We'd heard this word before, when others had tried to leave the church. *They are just deceived,* we'd thought sadly. *We are the one true church. Hopefully they will find their way back.*

But this time, things were different. It was as if a light bulb had come on, illuminating a once-darkened room, shining into all the cobwebby corners we'd never noticed before. Instead of feeling certain about our future in the Mormon Church, we felt only more uncertain the more we prodded and poked. We were both tired of being weighed down, tired of always trying so hard to do the right thing, yet winding up empty at the end of the day.

We'd both struggled with failed identities for far too long. I wanted what I'd seen in my new Christian friends — an intimate, genuine relationship with Jesus Christ.

Drew and I prayed together, asking God for the absolute truth. "Show us what is true, God. We are ready to follow you."

And I believe God did just that. He showed us the absolute truth — himself. He opened our hearts and minds and revealed what we'd started to believe. He was the one and only way. We did not need to follow a set of rituals and regulations to enter into a relationship with him, nor did we need to spend the rest of our lives trying to earn his grace or favor. Righteous deeds and acts of service were not the answer, either, because no matter how many we performed, we still never felt good enough to earn a place with God. We needed only to rest in Jesus Christ, give our hearts to him and surrender to his love. There were no gimmicks, no strings attached, no more exhausting ping-pong games with God. There was only grace.

Wow! This grace is scandalous. It is unwarranted. This isn't cheap grace — it's expensive! It is paid for with the blood of Jesus. I don't deserve it, no matter what I do. This is brilliant!

I read the book *Captivating* by Stasi Eldredge, and like Drew, I learned about my struggle for identity. I'd spent a lifetime never feeling good enough, despite my dutiful ways. My eating disorder had plagued me, my father's abuse and my mother's criticism echoing in my ears every time I starved myself. But it was never really about the food. It was about being noticed, about being loved. And as Eldredge pointed out, every girl longs to be truly seen and known and cherished. I had never felt seen or known. Instead, I had tried to find identity as a wife and mother in the Mormon Church. But the ache in my heart, the longing for true intimacy, had never gone away. Now I knew it was Jesus who could fill that ache. He was the missing piece I'd been searching for my whole life.

When we told our family we were leaving the Mormon Church, they took the news surprisingly well, but they still had questions.

"We understand you are on this journey, but why do you need to leave the church?"

Next, we told our best friends, who were Mormon. They didn't take the news as well. After we left their house, they let us know they wanted nothing to do with us or our kids anymore. While devastated, we remained strong.

"God, we are doing this for you, not for anyone else. We surrender to you," Drew and I prayed.

We met some new friends who took us to Church on the Rock, where they attended. We were overjoyed to attend and immediately felt at ease. We had lunch at their house after church, and they invited us to the church summer family camp.

"We'd love to go, but we don't have the money," we told them.

"Our church can offer you scholarships," our friends insisted. "We really want you to go!"

We agreed to go, and it proved to be one of the most amazing weeks of our lives. We met several wonderful couples who immediately felt like family. *This is what true intimacy feels like,* I realized. *Sharing our deepest feelings, our desires, our joys and sorrows. I feel like I've known these people forever!*

On our last night at camp, Drew told me he wanted to get baptized, proclaiming his new relationship with God to everyone. We trekked down to the lake with flashlights in hand, and the pastor dunked Drew in the chilly waters. Drew emerged sopping wet and smiling. *This is it, the beginning of our new journey,* I realized excitedly. *There's no turning back now!*

After returning home, I felt we needed to get rid of anything that represented our Mormon faith. We invited some friends over and did a four-hour bonfire, burning everything from Mormon baptism records to a library of literature to décor representing our old faith. As I watched the flames leap up and destroy the remnants of our past, my heart sang for joy. *Freedom, this is what we've finally found! There is no more bondage now!*

A few days later, I felt I needed to fully denounce my Mormon faith. I went out into the forest and began walking. As I raised my hands above my head, I began praying out loud.

"God, I am so grateful for what you've done! I surrender. I have been insecure and sad and full of pride. I denounce the Mormon Church. Remove all ties in the name of Jesus and free me!" As I prayed, the sun peeked through the trees, as though God smiled upon me. My heart swelled with happiness as I praised God for calling me out of the darkness and into the light. *I have no more fear, God! You are healing me, showing me your truth, making me new in you! Thank you!*

Drew and I remarried each other in a beautiful ceremony, surrounded by more than 100 friends. I wore a beautiful vintage lace dress my friend gave me, reciting meaningful vows to my husband in a gorgeous wedding barn. Afterward, we played worship music, and everyone sang. Someone anonymously donated the money for the event, and we praised God for his provision.

This is your party, God. You get all the glory here.

This is the beginning of our new life. And I can't wait to see what comes next.

஝஝஝

It was roughly 8 p.m. when Drew and I drove home from a family gathering. The summer sun had just started to set, a beautiful scene before us. The kids slept peacefully in the backseat, worn out from a long day. As I glanced to the left, I took in the glorious sunset, the striking display of clouds, and I smiled a little. *God, I know you made that. But I need you to do better. I need to know that you love me.*

I sat in silence as the car hummed along. And then I saw it, and my jaw dropped. There, in the sky, I saw my name written in the clouds. *Abigail.* There was no mistake.

It was my name, clear as could be. Stunned and overjoyed, I stared in disbelief.

Holy cow, am I really seeing this?

"Keep driving!" I cried to Drew, not wanting to miss the view as we neared the house.

Drew kept driving, and I took it all in, thanking God for showing up in the clouds. *I know this is from you, a gift just for me. A reminder of your love. Oh, thank you, God, for reminding me that I am yours!*

When we returned home, I put the kids to bed, then grabbed my journal. "God knows me, and he knows my name," I wrote, tears pricking my eyes. *He knows my name! I have a new identity in Christ. I am his beautiful bride, cherished and loved just as I am.*

Drew and I broke free from a faith that we came to believe held us in bondage to false teachings, and we cherished our newfound relationship with Jesus Christ. We loved attending Church on the Rock, where we met some of the most genuine people around. We came to love Pastor Bill, who we believe has a true heart for his people. We were still surrounded by imperfect, broken folks like ourselves, but we have found safety here. At last, we felt free to be vulnerable, to be our true selves and to admit we didn't have it all together. We felt free to love one another, encourage one another and pray for one another. It felt so unlike our former life, which revolved around good works and false pretenses.

Most importantly, Drew and I discovered grace. Though God delivered Drew from his sexual addiction and me from my eating disorder, we still struggled with various temptations and issues. But we started to understand something we did not appreciate before — grace is not cheap. Grace is free. Grace is not a game of ping-pong. We didn't need to keep wondering if we'd done enough to earn God's love. We confessed our sins to Jesus Christ, and because he died on the cross to pay for those sins, we believe we will spend eternity with him in heaven. We became more selfless, righteous, generous, forgiving and faithful, not because we wanted to qualify for God, but because we wanted to glorify God.

I love who Drew has become. I love who Christ has made me. And I know there is more growth to come.

I signed up for ballet lessons, something I always wanted to do. My lessons may not have worked out years before, but this time, nothing could stop me from dancing. And when I glided across the floor, I remembered the words to a song I wrote called "Is Grace Free?"

Sorrow and pain, bondage and strife
Have kept me from you all my life
Until you set me free and poured your grace on me
You came to save me, when I could not see you clearly
You paid the price of sins I've made
You laid down your life, you so freely gave
There's nothing I can do, no dark or light
I'm rescued by you, you came to fight my fight!

And then I danced some more.

BRAVE NEW DAY
THE STORY OF AVA AND RAYNE
WRITTEN BY ALEXINE GARCIA

Rayne

I walked in the door after school and headed straight for my room. I sank onto my bed and let the tears spill down my face and onto my pillow.

"You are so brave, Rayne."

"I can't imagine going through what you have gone through."

"You are my hero, Rayne."

I thought about all the encouragement I'd been given over the years. But in that moment, none of it seemed to help. Starting sixth grade in a new school was harder than I'd thought. I missed my old school and my old friends.

I sighed, rising from my bed and catching my reflection in the mirror. My thin hair was a reminder of the cancer. For three years, I'd tried wearing wigs to hide my secret, but wearing a wig was uncomfortable.

Sixth grade was going to be different. *If people don't like me because I have thin hair, I'll be okay. People don't have to like me,* I reminded myself. My heart ached, but I knew I would get through this. I'd been through much harder things.

❧❧❧

Ava

Life really couldn't be any better, I thought as I looked over at my husband. It felt like our love for each other grew daily. We had two beautiful children. Our 3-month-old son, Cole, lay on the bed flailing his little arms as I tried to pull a shirt over his head. We planned to spend some time at the park as a family since Luke had a day off. I went to Rayne's room and knelt next to her while she played with her dolls. *She looks like a little angel,* I thought as I took in her sweet blond pixie cut. I had just taken her to get a haircut for her 2nd birthday.

Luke held Cole as Rayne played on the carpeted floor. She got up and rubbed her little bum. "Ow, Mommy," she said, trying hard to remove her little red overalls. She was obviously uncomfortable.

"Do you have a rash, sweetheart? C'mon, baby, let's change that diaper."

I tickled Rayne's feet as I reached for wipes and cream. Suddenly during the changing process, I felt a bump on her behind. *Oh, no.* My heart stopped as the worst conclusion ran through my mind, *She has a tumor.*

As soon as I could, I snatched up my phone and called my sister-in-law. She had five kids, and there wasn't much she hadn't seen.

She came over right away and carefully laid Rayne down and felt the bump. "I think she'll be fine. Just take her to the doctor on Monday." A deep-seated fear came over me that I just could not shake.

After the appointment on Monday, I felt better. The

doctor told us it looked like our daughter had an abscess that needed to be drained. We gave her antibiotics and took her to a clinic for the outpatient procedure.

Luke and I sat in the waiting room during what we expected to be minor surgery. But when Dr. Wiles came through the double doors and walked toward us, I felt my heart catch in my throat. Everything slowed down as he stopped in front of us, pulled off his surgical hat and gave us a pensive look.

"The abscess is not what we initially thought," he said. "The bump is a tumor that we believe is cancer. I've already taken a biopsy and sent it to my friend Dr. Reese at Doernbecher Children's Hospital."

I collapsed back into my chair. *Did I just hear him right?*

"Come back tomorrow for a few more tests."

I clung to the hope that the biopsy would show the bump wasn't cancer or that it was benign.

A few friends and relatives came by the next morning and prayed for us and for Rayne. The way they talked to God about what was happening made me feel strong, even though the world seemed turned upside down. Luke and I drove Rayne back to the hospital the next morning in a fog. Neither of us said very much. We found our way to the oncology clinic. It was cold and white, and my heart began to break as I stood in the doorway. In the middle of the room was a crib with high metal bars. I thought about sweet little Rayne's room at home and the stark difference with this place. She had fluffy chenille blankets and a painting of the beach over her bed. This room was cold and sterile. My mind began to repeat, *I want to take you out of here and just run away.*

We waited as one doctor or nurse after another came and went. They poked Rayne with needles, connected beeping monitors to her skin and took samples for multiple tests. Doernbecher Children's Hospital in Portland was a teaching hospital where many physicians conducted their residencies. Each doctor who came in Rayne's room had something different to say. One would confirm his suspicions of cancer, while another would look at charts and examine Rayne and come up with a completely different diagnosis. Our emotions bounced between hope and despair.

As the examinations continued, Rayne yelled, "No, Mommy, no!" over and over. "Ow, Mommy!" escaped her lips with each needle prick. She looked at me with teary eyes that begged me to stop the pain. I felt helpless and wondered how much more we could take.

With the words of one kind doctor, my whole world suddenly shattered. "Rayne has Rhabdomyosarcoma, cancer of the soft tissue."

Luke sat in a chair next to Rayne's bed. He looked up at me, and I saw the same fear in his eyes that I felt. I walked over and sat on the arm of the chair, and he wrapped his arms around me. *How did we get here?* I thought to myself. *Three days ago, everything was perfect.* Luke and I silently suffered together.

A baseball-sized tumor was growing in her pelvis and

pushing on her bladder and rectum. Thankfully, the cancer had not spread to the rest of her body. She would need surgery soon.

Our family came and visited over the next two weeks. They sat in the room and helped us fill the monotonous hours. I felt far away when they talked about things like their new dog, going on vacation or getting the car detailed. I longed to go back to the perfect life Luke and I had built for ourselves.

The doctors successfully removed the large tumor. However, we learned that, due to the tumor's size, Rayne also would need aggressive chemotherapy.

A team entered the room wearing protective clothing from head to toe, including gloves and a facemask because the medicine was so toxic. They hung a bag on an IV line, and we watched as the poison flowed into our baby's body. The doctor read us a long list of side effects: "hair loss, mouth sores, shortness of breath, fatigue …"

I wanted to take Rayne out of there. I wanted to fight the cancer for her, to take her place. I didn't feel strong anymore. I began to talk to God relentlessly. *Help us. Let me be sick, and let her be well. Please, God, just heal her.*

Over the next six months of treatments, we would spend one week in the hospital, then three weeks at home. The side effects affected Rayne's tiny body in waves. We felt helpless as our little girl continuously shed silent tears.

At times, I blamed myself. *Is this my fault, God? Did I do something wrong?* I felt so much distance between him and me, but I continued to plead with him, anyway. When

RESCUE

Rayne stopped eating for three months, I begged God for healing. But I didn't let go of hope.

༄ ༄ ༄

My brother-in-law ran the buzzing clippers over her head as she giggled. When her head was soft and smooth, he went over to the mirror and buzzed his off, too. She joined him in front of the mirror and laughed at her reflection. "I look like a boy, Uncle Mark!"

My husband reached for the clippers and shaved his own head. "You look awesome, Rayne! Now we can be bald together!"

She was so beautiful. But, to me, even while she was covered with tubes in the hospital, she looked beautiful.

It was refreshing to see her smile and giggle.

For the most part, her smile and even her voice were absent. She would lay in her room so quiet and still. No coaxing could get her to play outside or eat small snacks. So even brief moments filled with smiles were like rays of light during a terrifying storm.

As the months passed, we spent more time in the hospital. Any little fever or cold caused her body to break down. Her immune system was nearly nonexistent because of the chemo treatments. Then one morning, Rayne's face looked puffy, and her skin turned yellow. We knew something was wrong. Thankfully, we were already at the hospital.

"Your daughter's liver is not functioning, and her

lungs are filling with fluid. She is very, very sick," the doctor told us. Within minutes, a team of nurses whisked her away to the Intensive Care Unit.

I sat in the ICU holding my son. The noises were different there, and an intensity buzzed in the air. But as I sat watching my little girl sleep, hooked up to all kinds of monitors, a peace came over me. Suddenly, I felt like God was actually listening to me. I could feel the peace of God for the first time.

Our family and friends visited often. "God is a comforter, and he loves to heal his people," one person would say.

"Our father is taking care of you," another would whisper with tear-filled eyes. "God loves you, and he is carrying you through this. I just know it."

How do these people know these things? How can they talk about God so intimately?

A longing grew inside of me. *I want to have faith like these people, God.*

Day after day, I watched my daughter sleep through treatment in the ICU. "Why is she sleeping so much?" I asked a doctor.

"Kids are amazing," the doctor answered. "When the pain is too much, their little bodies just sleep. It's like God's protection over them."

I felt God stepping closer each day that passed. Then on December 1, we threw a party in the hospital for Rayne's last day of chemotherapy. I was ready to leave all of it behind us. We celebrated Christmas with a new vigor that year. We were so happy that our little girl was home and regaining her health.

Our hopes only rose higher after her follow-up MRI and CAT scan in March. All of the results came back great. I accepted the fact that we would be in the hospital for routine scans every three months. It was better than anything else we had experienced.

We returned in June, after Rayne turned 3, for the scans and waited on the results. I really wasn't ready for the news the doctors had for us. A slow-motion moment happened again as the doctor told us, "There is a tumor growing again in the same spot. We are going to have to start chemotherapy again."

My emotions immediately flew out of control. Anger rolled around inside of me, like a bowling ball crashing through pins. I stood staring at the doctor in utter shock. Luke's hand squeezed around mine, and I knew he was feeling the same way.

The doctor went on to explain that this time was going to be more aggressive because it was her second tumor. Not only was she going to need chemo and more surgery, but also radiation.

I looked down at my daughter smiling up at me. I could tell she had no idea what was happening. Her cheeks were full and pink again. Her eyes sparkled, and all her hair had grown back. The anger and rage growing in me did not subside.

During the days leading up to the treatment, I questioned God. *What did we do wrong? Did we not have enough faith?* Even with all of my anger, I held onto hope with a clenched fist. I had no choice.

The statistics were grim. We were told to expect the worst. The success rate for the treatment Rayne was receiving was only 30 percent. As the treatment continued, she fell back into a reclusive, quiet nature. Her smile faded, and her eyes stared out at the world with a hollow, glazed-over look.

Since the chemo was more intense, we had to take extra precautions to protect Rayne's immune system. Rayne had to be put in a special room that only Luke and I could enter. A simple cold now had the potential to kill her. Despite my grief that God was letting my baby go through this all over again, I could not stop believing. I felt that same love for God that first sprouted from all this pain. My sister's prayer, "In all things, praise the Lord!" began to make sense. There was a subtle beauty in these painful moments. I couldn't see how things were going to end up, but I felt like I could trust God.

The plan was four months of chemo, then two months of radiation. Her body returned to the strange sleep coma, and we sat by her side. The blood count of white cells and platelets was in the single digits each time the doctors checked. My angry fist clenched tighter around my hope.

People from church met us in the waiting room and prayed for us. They knew nothing they could do could help us, however, they believed God could. I couldn't help but feel that same longing as they spoke about God like someone they knew so personally. "He is a lover of souls, just reach out to him." These words didn't describe the God I grew up knowing. I was sure I hadn't worked hard enough to deserve his love.

Watching these people pray for us changed my prayers. *I want to know you like these people know you,* became the cry to God constantly on my lips.

During a stem cell transplant, I sat by Rayne's side in her quiet room listening to worship music. My daughter looked so small and weak. She seemed to be fading. The doctors called the procedure a stem cell rescue, but I wondered if it would help at all. *What if this is it?* I thought. *What if Rayne is about to die?*

Suddenly, I opened up my heart and fell to my knees. *Jesus, I want to be her mom. I don't want to have to live my life without her. But I'm giving her up to you. You know what's best. I know you are able to come change this story.*

As these mumbled words escaped my lips, peace flooded the room. This was the first time I had ever completely trusted God with what would happen to Rayne. In that moment, I felt God's answer. I felt him there in the room. It wasn't an audible voice, not even a whisper. It was more like a quiet thought. *Its okay, you can trust her with me. I'll take care of her.*

I believed then that God had been carrying me and my family. He'd been watching over us since the day Rayne had been diagnosed. His love for me wasn't dependent on the good, or not so good, things I'd done. He loved my family and loved Rayne more than I ever could.

From that moment on, something changed. I wasn't the only one who was rescued. In the days that followed, Rayne's blood cell count slowly crept higher and higher. She was getting better.

We returned home after this treatment sequence on January 1 — 13 months after Rayne finished her first round of chemo — and celebrated a late Christmas together. As we sat together and opened gifts, it was as though Jesus was there in the room with us. The gifts we shared with each other were nice, but the real gift was having our family all together.

My prayers changed to conversation with a father who was constantly by my side. As the years passed, I realized that I was even more committed to Christ, and there was no going back. I no longer had to wonder about what was going to happen next. The Bible spoke of asking and seeking and God providing. I became so good at seeking. In return, God revealed so much to me. Looking back at that second bout of cancer, I know without a doubt that God healed my little girl's fragile body. The medicine and treatment did its work, but I believe it was God's hand pushing it all forward.

෴෴෴

Rayne

Even though I was happy with my decision to leave the wig at home, it wasn't easy. After school, I sat at the edge of my bed waiting for the tears to stop. No one at school talked to me. I spent my lunch hour alone. All of my old friends were together at a different school. At my new school, I was alone. I'd never had trouble making new friends before. For the entire first month of sixth grade, I longed for friends who knew me.

One night, Mom held my hand as we prayed together. As we finished, I looked up and saw my mom smiling at me. "I'm just going to have to be brave," I told her as tears rolled down my cheeks. "I can't do this on my own, but I have God by my side."

One night, I reluctantly went with my parents to a prayer meeting. I didn't want to be there and thought about getting home to get my homework done.

In the middle of the meeting, a friend said she had encouragement from God for me. "I wanted to tell you that when you're all alone and you feel like you're struggling in life, what feels like rejection is only God's protection. There are reasons for everything you've been through. I want you to know that you're a leader and that God's going to use your life to lead others to Christ. In order to do that, you need to spend time reading the Bible and asking God for guidance. You need to do that so when you go through hard times, you can be ready to face them."

I got through the sixth grade with lots of tears and struggles. But I kept true to my word, and I put on my brave face every day. I held on so tight to my friend's words.

I even painted the phrase, "What feels like rejection is

only God's protection," on my bedroom wall. I really could feel his protection that school year.

In the seventh grade, God answered my prayer for a few genuine friends. I met three girls who loved God like I did. They treated me like I was any other kid in school.

My cousin and I learned about a Christian conference called Wreckless Love happening in Hawaii, so we raised the funds and made plans to fly on our own for the first time in our lives. That summer, my cousin flew in from South Africa to meet me. We got on a plane together and seemed to land in a different world. The conference was an amazing experience. We loved spending time in such a beautiful place learning more about our faith and growing close to God.

I looked at all the other teens in the crowded conference hall on the third day. There wasn't an empty seat. Everyone came from different places all over the United States — people of different ages and ethnicities were all packed into one room.

This truth became even more real as all the girls moved into a different room. That day's conference focused on the concepts of beauty and identity. I looked around and saw so many people. There were girls of all nationalities, all beautiful in their own ways. I just knew that something huge was about to happen.

We gathered around and sang worship songs. When we were encouraged to pray for each other, some of the youth leaders began walking around the room and praying for us. One after the other stopped in front of me and prayed. The first girl had such a sincere smile. At first I was nervous, but as she prayed over me, I relaxed. When she was finished, she said, "You are perfectly beautiful just the way God made you. He will do great things through you."

Then the second youth leader walked up to me and prayed. She placed her hands on my shoulders, looked me in the eyes and said, "You are so beautiful just the way God made you, and God is going to do tremendous things in your life." I felt like God himself was reaching out to me as one person after another repeated the same message to me.

A sudden realization swam in my head. *It's true! God thinks I'm special. He thinks I am beautiful. He really, truly loves me.* I suddenly let myself cry. Really cry. It was as if I could feel the love of Jesus washing over me. I stood there with my hands raised, and tears flowed down my face. In that moment, I gave my life fully to him.

My parents had raised me in church, and I believed in God. It was a way of life for my family. But this beautiful experience was like looking God in the face. It was personal. It was a new beginning.

I came home with the confidence that God made me for a special purpose. I beat cancer for a purpose. I understood that God would use my story for something greater.

∽∽∽

I stood in front of the mirror and looked myself in the eyes. God healed my cancer, but I still wore reminders from it, even years later. I noted how I was smaller than most girls my age and took in the fact that my hair didn't look like everyone else's. But none of that mattered, because I learned that God thinks of me as truly beautiful. He has protected me since I was 2 years old battling cancer in a hospital crib. And he never stopped watching over me.

I realized I don't have to be afraid of what people may think or say. What once felt like rejection was only God's protection. I've had so many opportunities to share with others what God has done. He made me beautiful in more than just looks. I was so thankful that I had a beautiful story to tell.

HUNTING FOR LIFE
THE STORY OF RYAN
WRITTEN BY MARIE SHEPHERD

I carried my .30-30 Winchester rifle in one hand and pushed back the brush with my other. I hoped to get a glimpse of my prey. I made my way forward, intent on tracking that black-tailed buck.

Even in the cold of a Washington winter, sweat dripped off of my brow. I was determined to find what I came out here looking for. The drops slipped down into my eyes and challenged my vision.

I thought I caught a glimpse of a tail, but no. What kept me moving was the excitement of seeing fresh tracks. Nothing could calm my nerves as I hunted, and yet, this is the place where I always found peace.

At 14, I thought nothing would ever keep me from these woods. It's where I found freedom. It's where I learned to appreciate the simple beauty of nature. I knew so much waited out there for me to learn and discover.

I took a sharp left. My path was unmarked. As daylight began to fade, I had to find my own way back to my hunting buddy, Asher, who'd be waiting for me near the truck. This time, I would return empty-handed, with nothing but a smile to share with him. I didn't know how soon my carefree path would take a drastic turn.

RESCUE

"I'm pregnant." My girlfriend, Brittany, wouldn't look me in the eye. I could tell she was terrified.

"Are you sure?" Maybe she had made a mistake. Maybe she was just scared. She was still in high school — what did she know about being pregnant, anyway?

"Yes, Ryan! I am sure!" She probably hadn't even wanted to tell me.

I believed her and got scared, too. There would be no going back to how life used to be. This baby would change everything. Not only did I feel like high school was over, but so was the rest of my life. I had just begun to figure out what I wanted to be doing, where I wanted to go and who I wanted to be.

"Well, it's okay, Brittany." I tried to reassure us both with confidence I didn't entirely feel. "We can talk to my mom. She works at a pregnancy care center. I'm sure she can help you." Somebody needed to be in control of this situation. Someone needed to have answers. I longed to deliver the right words, to pull them out of a fresh-flowing stream like a slippery, wet salmon, alive and obvious.

My mind trailed off. *I wish you could eliminate this whole mess. I wish I could just go back into the forest, to where I feel free and alive.* I realized Brittany was glaring at me, her eyes cold. I knew for both our sakes, my thoughts would have to change.

આ આ આ

The boat ride from La Conner to Ketchikan seemed longer than it was. It dragged on, taking me from everything I'd ever known. Although I was excited about Alaska — the adventure and the money I was going to make on a commercial fishing boat — loneliness hit me before the boat even left the dock.

Time felt drawn out. Without my friends, without college classes, I had nothing but time on my hands. Time to think. Time to worry. Time alone. I got so lonesome, I even tried praying, although I wasn't sure why I attempted to or to what end.

The grueling work included long, sleepless hours fishing outside in the frigid air, constantly proving to the other crew members that I deserved to be there. I felt proud to work so hard to provide for my newborn daughter. At times I could almost feel myself maturing and getting more responsible. Then I'd wonder how much Cassie had grown in the months I'd been gone, since right after she was born.

☙☙☙

When I returned home, Brittany wouldn't let me see Cassie. I couldn't believe it. I had to fight for the legal right to see my daughter. I'd worked so long and so hard to financially support my precious baby girl, and it hurt to have to defend my paternity or my motives. But I submitted to a blood test, which proved that I was the father. It was such an ugly time. I even doubted my own intentions and my qualifications to be a dad — but I never questioned my love for Cassie.

I kept Cassie on the weekends. My time with her was always short, and I sensed that she was bonding with my mom better than she was with me.

I wanted to continue my education, especially with Cassie to consider, and decided that spending months away on a fishing boat wasn't going to work. As a student, I'd thought that maybe I could teach. The idea of being a teacher appealed to me more as time went on. I kept trying to track down something that would be a good fit for me.

As I hunted for my place in the world, one of my anthropology classes caught my attention. I quickly became enthralled by the Native American culture and way of life. I was drawn to living off the land, seeking simplicity and escaping all forms of materialism. I began hunting and fishing more than ever before. I began going deeper into the woods, sometimes getting lost, but always discovering something new: plants, mushrooms, berries.

I considered the difference between what I wanted in life and what I actually needed. When I was out in the woods, I knew I wanted to live off the land, to learn life skills and be able to make things so I could live without money. In my endeavors to master outdoor survival skills, I tried to carve something out of wood for the first time — and I was hooked. I loved working with my hands. I was entranced by the sound of the knife, the smell of the wood, by the fact that I could transform the wood that I found into a beautiful creation. I realized that I liked to express myself in this way. I was able to make something in my imagination become a reality.

I quickly became aware that if I wanted to use my newfound passion and talent to make a living from my art, I needed to become really good at it. I started to carve all day long in my parents' basement. I gathered my best examples and assembled a portfolio, complete with a letter about myself. I sent it out over and over again. And then I waited. And hoped.

I finally received this letter from a world-renowned artist:

> *Dear Ryan,*
>
> *I understand that you would like to learn this Native art form of carving. I have seen your examples, and I believe that you have great potential. I am inviting you to work under me as my apprentice. If you are willing to make the four-hour drive every week, as I understand you have your young daughter on the weekends, then you are welcome to begin immediately upon receiving this letter ...*

And so I began my apprenticeship. It was my first step toward pursuing a real career in Native American art, though I had no idea what would come from it.

ॐ ॐ ॐ

"Yes, I understand." I held the phone and began to tremble with anticipation.

"Of course, Ryan. I'd be honored to have you," he was saying in his calm Chinookan way.

"Thank you." I hoped my voice didn't betray my excitement.

"You are aware that this is a two-year commitment?"

Immediately, my mind went to my wife, Amy, then pregnant with our first child.

"Yes, I am aware of that." I couldn't put into words what a huge provision this would be for us or what a grand opportunity this would be for me as an artist.

"You know, Ryan, I did look at your portfolio. Your work is really very good." I could tell he meant every word. "At least," he added, "for a white guy."

It would be my first major public art commission. I was hired to work alongside the native Chinook Indian who had selected me to work on a project for the Lewis & Clark Bicentennial Commission. This opportunity became the turning point in my career.

This was a *big* deal. It meant two years of solid, steady income, for one thing. It also meant building a resume I could take pride in. I hoped not only to be trained personally by a master carver and learn all that I could from him, but also to establish respect as a non-native carver in the Northwest. This was the opportunity of my lifetime — the break I had been searching for and the beginning as an artist that I desperately needed.

ৡৡৡ

I shook my head to try to erase the memory, but it was still there, as real as the day it happened. My hands clenched the steering wheel as I drove to work. It had been a year since I started the plank house project, and too many things had been happening so close to home that were out of the ordinary: the tornado hitting the project site on the one day I wasn't present, then watching Mount St. Helens erupt and *then* my encounter with the old man no one else had seen before or since.

He walked right up to me while I was carving. Everyone else was busy doing other things. He said to me, "Son, you need to read the book of John."

I'd given him a blank stare. "I'm sorry?"

"You need to read the book of John. In the Bible." He nodded.

"Are you talking to me?" I looked around to see if anyone else could possibly be the intended audience.

"Yes, son. You need to know that God loves you." He smiled.

I smiled back, hesitantly. He nodded again and walked away, seemingly satisfied.

I never saw him again.

I shuddered at all the supernatural weirdness. I didn't know what to make of these crazy events.

When I had asked Ron about the old man, he didn't know what I was talking about.

"No, man, have you seen him before?" I was serious.

"What's up with you today?" Ron glanced at me.

I shook my head. I had asked Ron because he believed in things that were unexplainable.

"No. Promise." I pressed Ron for a genuine answer, and all he said was that maybe he was a spirit man.

"Like an angel or something?" I asked.

"Or something," Ron replied.

No one else seemed too concerned. I knew that the art form I pursued was spiritually loaded, but I was afraid. Afraid that I was not supposed to be a part of this project, afraid that maybe I shouldn't be doing this carving thing at all.

But I took a deep breath and chose to continue driving to work. This was my job. This was the opportunity I had been hunting for. This was the path I had chosen.

ॐ ॐ ॐ

"I am so ready for this vacation." I looked over at my dad as we sat down to drink coffee in the airport. I was glad it was just the two of us for a minute. "Things have been kind of tense for Amy and me lately."

My dad assured me, "Well, son, it's going to be the best part of the year. And right now you have nothing but Hawaii to enjoy." In his own way, my dad always tried to encourage me.

"Yeah, it will be good to get away and reflect some. I am glad to be where I'm at, Dad, don't get me wrong. Amy and I are in love, we are committed and we've grown up together. I just struggle with feeling like we're in different places in our lives, you know?" I stumbled over what I was trying to say.

"What do you mean, Ryan?" My dad was always so sincere.

"Well, Amy's been so into this Bible class thing and wanting to go to church and that's great for her, but I just don't know about all the changes it's brought for my life — all of our friends are different now ..." I was venting, and I knew it.

"Is that such a bad thing?" Dad smirked.

" ... and we have some financial stress that is really upsetting me, and Amy doesn't seem concerned, well, she isn't worried about it. Amy and I are in a good place between the two of us, but different places in life right now, I guess ..." I was trailing off. It looked like my dad had tuned out.

"Hey, I know that guy." I nodded toward the man reaching for his coffee order from the counter. He turned his head just in time to catch a glance.

"Hi, Ryan! It's been years. What are you doing here?" Surprise was written on his face as much as I'm sure it showed on mine.

"Ethan! Wow, hi! Uh, we are catching a flight to Hawaii. My wife, Amy, and I are taking a vacation with my parents this year."

"That's wonderful! My wife and I are also heading to the Islands. We're going to be staying in Kona. Maybe we'll see you there? It'd be fun to catch up after all this time. Let me give you my number." He reached in his pocket for a pen. I smoothed out a napkin. Talk about a chance meeting.

かかか

After meeting up with Ethan in Hawaii, he invited me to join him and his family at their cabin in Alaska on the Kenai River. The salmon run of legends. I felt a little awkward just joining in on their family vacation, but I liked Ethan and reminded myself he'd invited me. It would have been foolish to pass up the opportunity in Alaska. And after the crazy chance of meeting Ethan again on the way to Hawaii, I figured it was meant to be.

When I arrived at the cabin, I felt almost instantly something in the air up there. Everything was fresh and clean and beautiful. Ethan's whole family was absolutely wonderful. They were full of life and so open to share everything with me. They welcomed me like part of the family without any reservations.

As we sat by the campfire one night, Ethan's sister shared an incredible story of how she had been healed from a physical illness — no medical explanation for her instant healing. She claimed it was the power of praying and believing in Jesus.

Her husband, Tim, turned to me. "Hey, Ryan, do you go to church anywhere back in Washington?" It seemed like a natural question for him to ask. I balked a bit.

"Nah, not really into religion. I go out into the woods

— that's my church." I wanted to share what I felt was sacred to me.

Tim looked at me for a moment. There was no judgment in his voice. "You know, Ryan, the spiritual man needs to be rejuvenated." Even as he said it, his words resonated deep within me. They challenged me. I knew that in that moment Tim had shared his spirit with me. It seemed he had no fears. I wanted to know more about that kind of confidence. I wanted to be as free as Tim seemed to be.

I tried to return to the good feelings of the camaraderie surrounding me. I sighed with contentment in the campfire light. But at the same time, I also felt restless. Tim's question was like a song I could not get out of my head. His one simple reason nagged at me. It reminded me of why I loved hunting, tracking and fishing. And yet, I felt there was something more to what Tim meant when he said "rejuvenated."

❧❧❧

"Daddy's home!" Amy called for the kids. "How was Alaska?" My wife met me at the door expectantly. I looked at her as if somehow I was seeing her again for the first time.

"It was awesome. I want us to go to Ethan's church on Sunday." Amy looked at me quizzically. She probably thought I was joking.

"I've got to tell you all about Alaska and Ethan's

amazing family. He invited us to come to his church and meet his pastor. It sounds pretty cool." I knew Amy was pleased that I was the one suggesting we go to a church together. She'd been the one wanting to go for so long.

‍ ‍ ‍ 🙶🙶🙶

For me, visiting Church on the Rock for the first time was like the moment the deer you've been tracking crosses your path. It was meant to be. It was like an encounter I'd been waiting for, but I never even knew it.

It was a small church. I felt welcomed, I already knew a few people there and they were nice. But when the music started and people began to sing, it was like nothing I had ever experienced. A warm dizziness surged within me. Everyone was actively engaged. Sometimes it felt like everyone was swaying together, like salmon going upriver, as if we were all swimming in a sea of love. I had this upwelling of emotions, and all I knew was that I didn't want it to end.

"That was a trip! Did you *feel* that?" I asked Amy on the drive home.

"Yeah! I wanted to ask if *you* felt that." She was beaming. I was still mesmerized.

"What the heck was that?" I had to know. When Ethan's friend, the pastor, had shared his story that morning, it was like every word was exactly what I needed to hear. It was as if he was talking directly to me, and he didn't even know me.

"I don't know, do *you* want to go back?" She glanced my way.

"I want to go back. We have to go back!" I was hooked. I'd been around all the spiritualism of the native culture and exposed to feelings and things that were not of this world, as well as the people who sincerely believed in them. I had actually always doubted the spirit animals and discounted the myths.

But I sensed that *this God* they were talking about was *real*. He was as real as the wind I had felt on my skin, rushing past me, as I desperately tried to hold back the tears that were streaming down my cheeks as I stood in that church. It was just like Tim had described to me in Alaska — it *was* a place to go and rejuvenate my spirit.

After I got to know God a little bit more, I remembered a young man I encountered a few years before. He was a student of mine on a reservation. He drove up to meet me one day. He was 16 at the time. He was very interested in the art I taught. He wanted to understand more about the native ways reflected in my carving. He asked me about the native spirits and the spirit animals that they believed in. This guy wanted to know if they were real. I had wrestled with my answer. I told him no, the spirit animals were not real. I said there is only one real God. This young man was killed in a car accident only a few weeks after my conversation with him. I wondered if he had chosen to believe in God before he died.

Even after I began living a rejuvenated lifestyle, this

vivid memory challenged me to never forget that any time I saw someone might be the last. As I sought after God's character and made decisions to know him more, my opportunities to teach and preserve the native way of life still abounded. Teaching and carving were still my passion and talent. I was more grateful than ever for more time to decide how to keep using my gifts in this life.

২৯ ২৯ ২৯

I watched my old hunting buddy, Asher, die of cancer. He was my age. We went to high school together, but had drifted our separate ways. When I found him again through Facebook, he already had cancer. Toward the end of his life, we got to spend a lot of time together. I found out that he had been questioning God at the same time I had, so long before, when neither of us ever talked about those things. We both later wished we had discussed deep matters back then. But when you're young, you think you're the only one going through something.

We hunted together again before he died. Asher said he wasn't going to let his pain stop him. During his last days, Asher wanted to be closer to God. He longed to be in nature. We often went way out in the woods to just be together in the stillness. Sharing those times made us very close. We would talk and talk about God. Even when all was not right with Asher's world, he still had peace.

The thing I'd expected to see in Asher, I never did: fear. I always had an unexplainable fear of cancer, and I wasn't the one who was diagnosed with it. Here was my good friend literally dying from it, sometimes writhing in pain, and yet he was not afraid. Asher had joy. He said his faith was in God. He told me how he had never let religion keep him from Jesus. I truly saw that in his life. Even if someone close to him believed something differently than he did about God, it didn't shake his own faith.

In spite of Asher's death, I saw God in Asher's life. Through the heart-wrenching time of losing my good friend, I gained freedom from my lifelong fear of dying from cancer. The character of God, his love and joy and peace in Asher, enabled me to stop fearing death itself. By watching my friend actually die in peace, *I* was able to have peace.

Before Asher died, he asked me to be there for his brother Logan. Since Logan had lost his brother as a hunting companion, I volunteered to put in for a special hunt with him. The odds of getting picked were thousands to one. People put in for these hunts for years and years and never got chosen. But the very first time that Logan and I put our names in, we both got picked for two out of the three tags they were giving away. It was like winning the lottery.

We were both in awe. I pictured Asher up in heaven, pleased with himself for talking God into pulling that one off. Some called it luck. Others said it was just a coincidence. I remember Logan himself declared, "It was too much coincidence to be what some call luck." I agreed.

We set off together, just the two of us, to hunt elk for a

week. In the wake of Asher's passing, this was a precious time. We both needed each other, and we both needed God. I hoped and prayed that Logan would know how much Asher wanted him to experience God's love and the peace that he had lived and died with.

එඑඑ

While walking out into the beauty of nature — what I still saw as God's own cathedral — I started reflecting on Asher's death, and I'd come to realize a few more things about my own journey. I had searched for only one thing: simplicity. It was what I always wanted. Influenced by my wilderness survival days, my life and work always reflected that cry for freedom. Freedom from the fears I once had. Freedom from the burdens of doubt and stress and worries that so often weighed me down. All along, I had been looking for the traces of this kind of simple life, hunting for the peace I only truly found in a loving God and knowing that it was my love for God that gave my life meaning.

For me, finding faith was a process. Like carving a figure in a log, it progressed, bit by bit. My fear and anxiety didn't fall off all at once. Nor could I pinpoint a precise moment when I decided to follow Jesus. I came to know God just like I came to know my art — by doing it every day. My faith became a part of me, bit by bit. As I learned more, I put more into practice. I think of it as God revealing himself to me in the same way that I searched for him, a little at a time.

CONCLUSION

What do we make of the falls we take in life?

Over the years, I have spoken with hundreds of individuals exploring the ideologies and supposed doctrines of the Christian church. I have asked them what they hold against Christianity or what they have perceived Christianity to be. Most repeat variations of the same theme: "I can't believe in a God who would allow Auschwitz, Columbine or Cambodia. My Christian friend died of cancer despite all of the Christian prayers. The majority of people in countries like India went to bed hungry last night — how can you reconcile that with a loving God?"

A well known German pastor and theologian, Helmut Thielicke, after an extended tour of the United States, made the observation that American Christians "have an inadequate view of suffering." I would add that Americans in general have not adequately thought through their questions on suffering, injustice or even the consequences of personal negative behavior. If the Creator has given his creation free will, it would be quite illogical to blame him for their actions or hold him responsible for the results.

The reality is that we do live in an imperfect, marred and "fallen" world. Every religion, from Buddhism to Zionism, must address the problem of suffering. What difference does Christian faith make? What resources can the Christian fall back on? If you are in the state of falling or have completely crashed, it is probably the question on your mind: How does God care about my situation? *Does* he care?

I have found that searching and examining the claims of the scriptures, and in particular, the life of Jesus Christ, will reveal some very interesting observations. The fact that Jesus came to earth where he suffered and died does not remove pain from our lives. But it does, in fact, show that God did not sit idly by and watch us suffer in isolation. As the words to the pop song ask, "What if God were one of us? Just a stranger on the bus?" He did become one of us! In Jesus, God gives us an up-close and personal look at his response to human suffering. All of our questions about God and human suffering should be filtered through what we know about Jesus Christ, which provokes the question: What do you know about Jesus Christ? *Really?*

How did God in the flesh respond to pain, trouble and people who had fallen? When he met a person who was hurting, he was deeply moved. Not ever did he say, "Endure your hunger! Swallow your grief!" When his friend Lazarus died, he wept with grief. Every time he was directly asked, he healed the pain. He often broke laws to do so, as when he touched the woman with a hemorrhage of blood or when he touched the outcast with leprosy, ignoring the man's contagious state.

The question "Does God care?" is not one that tormented Jesus' disciples. They had evidence of his compassion every day; they saw what he did and could look at his face.

When Jesus himself faced suffering and endured the punishment for all of the falls and sin we would ever commit, what was his response? He recoiled from it like we all do.

He experienced that most human sense of abandonment: "My God, my God, why have you forsaken me?" Jesus, on his last night on the planet, experienced fear, helplessness and apprehension — the same emotions we all experience in our suffering and seeking. The record of Jesus' life should forever answer the questions "How does God feel about our falls?" and "When is he going to cut us a break or 'throw us a line'?"

He did not give us some abstract doctrine or set of rules to live by; he gave us himself. Other philosophies and religions may explain away difficult things, but have no power to change them. The Gospel, the story of Jesus Christ, promises change — change you have read about, change that is evidenced by the reality of transformed lives.

Jesus Christ is God's lifeline to mankind. Jesus Christ is God's lifeline to you.

"This is good and acceptable in the sight of God our Savior, who desires all men to be saved and to come to knowledge of the truth. For there is one God, and one mediator also between God and men, the man Christ Jesus, who gave himself as a ransom for all" (1 Timothy 2:3-6).

"The Lord is not slow about his promise, as some count slowness, but is patient toward you, not wishing for any to perish, but for all to come to repentance" (2 Peter 3:9).

"For the wages of sin is death, but the free gift of God is eternal life in Christ Jesus our Lord" (Romans 6:23).

Jesus Christ makes a very simple but profound promise to you in the Bible: "Truly, truly, I say to you, he who believes has eternal life" (John 6:47).

This is so simple that it is very easy to stumble over it. You mean that by just believing, no more, no less, I can be saved? Absolutely!

Listen to what the Apostle Paul said in the book of Romans: "If you confess with your mouth Jesus as Lord, and believe in your heart that God raised him from the dead, you will be saved; for with the heart a person believes, resulting in righteousness, and with the mouth he confesses, resulting in salvation" (Romans 10:9-10 NASB).

You can pray a simple prayer like the one below, and if it is from your heart, the Lord will certainly hear you and answer at this moment.

Lord Jesus, I know I have sinned and come short of your expectations for my life. I confess my sins to you today. Thank you for sending Jesus to die for me and pay the penalty for my sins. Come into my heart, and be my Savior and Lord. Thank you for saving me. Amen.

CONCLUSION

If you prayed this prayer, then congratulations on your decision! We at Church on the Rock would love to hear from you. We would be glad to answer any questions you may have about the Christian life. You can contact us through the contact information inside the back cover of this book.

With Christ's Love,
Pastor Bill Courtnay
Church on the Rock

We would love for you to join us at Church on the Rock!

We meet Sunday mornings at 8a.m.,
10 a.m. and 12 p.m.

We are located at
500 SW Eaton Blvd
Battle Ground, WA 98604

Contact Information
Phone: 360.723.0723
Website: www.rockwa.com
Email: churchontherockwa@gmail.com

For more information on reaching your city with
stories from your church, go to
www.testimonybooks.com.

GOOD CATCH
PUBLISHING